BATHROOM TRIVIA

WRITTEN BY MAX BRALLIER
ILLUSTRATED BY JIM STOTEN

LONDON, NEW YORK,
MELBOURNE, MUNICH, and DELHI

Author Max Brallier
Illustrator Jim Stoten
Project Editor Alexander Cox
Project Designer Jess Bentall

Editors Wendy Horobin, Joe Harris,
Ben Morgan, and Lorrie Mack
Designers Gemma Fletcher, Hedi Hunter,
Poppy Joslin, and Lauren Rosier
Production Editor Sean Daly
Production Controller Claire Pearson
Jacket Designer Jess Bentall
Jacket Editor Mariza O'Keeffe
US Editor Margaret Parrish
Publishing Manager Bridget Giles
Art Director Rachael Foster
Category Publisher Mary Ling

First published in the United States in 2009
by DK Publishing
375 Hudson Street, New York, New York 10014

Printed and bound by WKT, China

Discover more at
www.dk.com

CONTENTS

CONTENTS

FAMOUS
FIRSTS & LASTS

1ST PLACE
FIRST BIG MAC

In 1968, Pittsburgh McDonald's owner Jim Delligatti noticed local Big Boy restaurants selling double-decker burgers. McDonald's HQ let him experiment with the formula, and soon he had two burgers, cheese, pickles, onions, lettuce, and special sauce—the world's first Big Mac!

FIRST BOTTLE OF COCA-COLA

1ST PLACE

Invented by pharmacist John Pemberton, the first bottle of Coca-Cola was sold on May 8, 1886, at Jacob's Pharmacy in Atlanta.

FIRST TRANSATLANTIC SOLO FLIGHT BY A WOMAN

1ST PLACE

In 1932, Amelia Earhart became the first woman to fly solo across the Atlantic Ocean. It took her 15 hours.

LAST QUEEN OF FRANCE

LAST PLACE

Maria Antonia Josefa Joanna von Habsburg-Lothringen, better known as Marie Antoinette, was the last queen of France. In 1793, during the French Revolution, she was tried for treason and executed by guillotine. She was 37 years old.

FIRST MICKEY MOUSE CARTOON

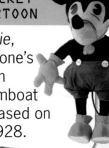

Steamboat Willie, featuring everyone's favorite cartoon mouse as a steamboat captain, was released on November 18, 1928.

LAST CONCORDE FLIGHT

The supersonic Concorde airliner made its last flight, from New York to London, on October 24, 2003.

FIRST MAN ON THE MOON

On July 21, 1969, American astronaut Neil Armstrong became the first person to set foot on the Moon. He made the famous statement, "That's one small step for man, one giant leap for mankind."

LAST DODO BIRD

The dodo was a flightless, goofy-looking bird that lived on the island of Mauritius, off the coast of Africa. The last dodo died in 1681.

LAST BEATLES CONCERT

The last time John, Paul, George, and Ringo all performed together on stage was August 29, 1966, at Candlestick Park in San Francisco. The stadium was just about half full. Imagine the crowd if people had known it was to be their last concert!

FIRST ITEM SOLD ON EBAY

The first item sold on eBay was sold by the company's founder, Pierre Omidyar, in 1995. He successfully auctioned off a busted laser pointer for $14.

9

ALL ABOUT DINOSAURS

FAST RUNNER
Velociraptor means "swift thief."

MR. NASTY
Tyrannosaurus rex is the most famous of all the dinosaurs. The name means "tyrant lizard king"—so you know he was tough. The average tyrannosaur was 40 ft (12 m) long, 20 ft tall (6 m), and weighed about 8 tons (6.5 tonnes).

HORN FACE
The *Triceratops* is instantly recognizable because of its short nasal horn and the two big horns on top of its head. The name *triceratops* literally means "three-horned face."

Scientists think the *Bruhathkayosaurus* was the biggest of all the dinosaurs—at 140 feet long (43 m) and weighing 220 tons (200 metric tons).

NOT SO SCARY
The smallest dinosaur was the *Compsognathus*—it was about the size of a chicken!

SPACE DINOSAURS?
Yep—there are dinosaurs in space—although we're the ones who put them there. In 1998, a fossil *Coelophysis* skull was taken to the Mir space station on the space shuttle *Endeavour*.

Dinosaurs were reptiles that lived between 220 million and 65 million years ago, during the Triassic, Jurassic, and Cretaceous periods of geological time. In movies and on TV you usually just see the big, crazy-looking ones. But there were all kinds of dinosaurs—big ones, small ones, herbivores (plant eaters), and carnivores (meat eaters).

SCARIEST DINOSAUR
Most people think the *Velociraptor* was the most dangerous of the dinosaurs, but that's not true. The *Utahraptor* was even worse than *Velociraptor*. It was one of the most vicious and lethal killing machines that ever walked on Earth. It was larger than the *Velociraptor* and had even bigger claws.

It's one of the biggest questions in science—what caused the extinction of the dinosaurs? Well, no one knows for sure. But scientists suspect that a giant asteroid crashed into Earth and kicked up so much dust and dirt into the atmosphere that it blocked the sunlight and the climate changed. The dinos couldn't handle the changes, and eventually died out.

SMARTY PANTS
In comparison to its relatively small body size, the *Troodon* had the biggest brain of any dinosaur.

11

FALSE OR FALSE?

THE TRADITIONAL CHINESE DESSERT IS A FORTUNE COOKIE

False. Fortune cookies were invented in the United States in around 1918 by a Chinese immigrant, George Jung.

SWEAT SMELLS BAD

False. Sweat has no odor. It's the bacteria that live and thrive on the sweat that smell bad. Soap and water get rid of the bacteria, so don't forget those armpits!

"FALSE OR FALSE?"

BULLS GET ANGRY AT THE COLOR RED

False. Actually, bulls are color-blind. As far as they're concerned, you could be waving a nice blue plaid at them.

"FALSE OR FALSE?"

HOLLYWOOD LEADS IN THE MOVIE WORLD

False. India produces three times as many movies as Hollywood every year.

CATS ALWAYS LAND ON THEIR FEET

False. It's true that cats have a great sense of balance, but they can be badly injured in falls from any height. So—NO—you can't drop your neighbor's cat off the roof.

GEORGE WASHINGTON HAD WOODEN TEETH

False. George had the best teeth available in those days, crafted from walrus ivory.

"FALSE OR FALSE?"

PEOPLE WHO WON'T LOOK YOU IN THE EYE WHEN THEY TALK ARE UNTRUSTWORTHY

False. Psychologists have discovered that con artists and habitual liars are more likely to maintain steady eye contact than any other group of people.

THE "HOLLYWOOD" SIGN WAS PUT UP TO PROMOTE THE FILM INDUSTRY

False. It was put up in 1924 to promote a real estate development called "Hollywoodland." In 1945, when the sign was starting to deteriorate, the city of Hollywood took it over, fixed the first nine letters, and dumped the last four.

CREATURES
FROM THE DEEP

JOKES!
Q: Why are fish so smart?
A: Because they live in schools!

Q: Why is it so easy to weigh fish?
A: They have their own scales!

The **BLUE WHALE** is the largest animal on Earth. They can weigh up to 180 tons (160 metric tons). The largest ever measured was almost 100 ft (30 m) long! The **HEART** of a blue whale is about the size of a Volkswagen car!

THE WHISTLE of the blue whale is the loudest sound produced by any animal on Earth. Lucky they don't live next door!

The **GIANT PACIFIC OCTOPUS** is the largest octopus in the world. The largest one ever caught weighed 600 lb (272 kg) and had tentacles measuring 30 ft (9 m)!

An **OCTOPUS** has 3 hearts.

GOLDFISH can live for decades—so take good care of that thing! The oldest known pet goldfish ever, "Goldie," lived to be 45 years old.

FLYING FISH don't actually fly—they glide on wind currents above the surface of the water, sometimes up to 20 ft (6 m) above the waves!

In **JAPAN**, electric eels have been used to power **CHRISTMAS** trees!

There are more than **25,000 IDENTIFIED** species of fish in Earth's oceans—and scientists estimate that there are about **15,000 SPECIES** that are still to be found!

A baby fish is called a **FRY**.

The **SMALLEST FISH** in the world is the Philippine goby—it's less than ⅓ in (0.8 cm) when fully grown.

SHARKS are the most feared of the underwater creatures. In reality, they kill only about 10 people a year. Deer kill about 100 people a year, and coconuts kill about 150 a year. So relax about the sharks—**FEAR THE COCONUT!**

Starfish have **EIGHT EYES**—one at the end of each tentacle. But no brain or heart!

SEAHORSES tend to mate under a full Moon. How romantic! Then it's the males who carry the babies and give birth!

CRAZY COINCIDENCES

LIFE IS FULL OF LITTLE QUIRKS AND COINCIDENCES! BUT SOME ARE JUST INCREDIBLE AND, QUITE FRANKLY, BIZARRE!

> "THE MOST ASTONISHINGLY INCREDIBLE COINCIDENCE IMAGINABLE WOULD BE THE COMPLETE ABSENCE OF ALL COINCIDENCES."
>
> John Allen Paulos, Mathematician

SHIPWRECKED

IN 1885, PLAYWRIGHT ARTHUR LAW WROTE CAROLINE, A PLAY ABOUT A MAN NAMED ROBERT GOLDING, THE SOLE-SURVIVOR OF A SHIPWRECK. JUST DAYS AFTER THE PLAY'S OPENING NIGHT, A SHIP NAMED THE CAROLINE SANK AND ONE MAN SURVIVED—ROBERT GOLDING.

Lightning strikes thrice!

In 1899, a man in Taranto, Italy, was standing in his backyard when he was struck and killed by a bolt of lightning. Thirty years later, his son was killed in the exact same spot—again, by a bolt of lightning. Then, in 1949, Rolla Primarda, the grandson of the first man and the son of the second, was struck and killed by a bolt of lightning in the exact same spot.

Just lying around...

In 1973, actor Anthony Hopkins was to appear in an adaptation of the book *The Girl From Petrovka*—but couldn't find a copy of the book anywhere. He then found one lying on a bench at a train station. It turned out to be the author's own copy that he had loaned to a friend, who had lost it!

CRAZY!

LUCKY KID

A man named Joseph Figlock was walking down a Detroit street in the 1930s when a baby fell from a window. Luckily, Figlock broke the baby's fall and they were both unharmed. Then, a year later, the exact same baby fell—and landed on Joseph Figlock! Again, they were both unharmed.

BIGGEST...

Too fast to catch, too slow to notice, too big to handle, or too small to see? Here's a list of all these things and more...

Biggest Burrito—In 1997, California restaurants joined together to create the world's largest burrito. When finished, it measured 3,578 ft (1,090 m) long and weighed the same as a White Rhinoceros— 4,456 lb (2,021 kg). Hope they were hungry.

Biggest Book—*Bhutan: A Visual Odyssey Across the Last Himalayan Kingdom* by Michael Halley is nearly the size of a Ping-Pong table and weighs more than 130 lb (60 kg)!

FASTEST
SLOWEST

Fastest Production Car— Bugatti Veyron. With 1,001-brake-horsepower, this pricey car ($1,200,000) goes from 0-60 mph (0-96 km/h) in 2.46 seconds, and has a hair-raising top speed of 253 mph (407 km/h)!

Slowest Animal— Not counting sea creatures like sponges, which don't move at all (lazy bones), the slowest animal in the world is the sloth.

SMALLEST

Biggest Man-Made Structure—For centuries, the biggest man-made structure on Earth was the Great Wall of China. But today, it's the Fresh Kills landfill in New York. At its peak, it towered a staggering 75 ft (23 m) taller than the Statue of Liberty. That's a LOT of garbage.

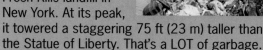

Biggest Baby—She ain't heavy, she's my sister. Nadia Khalina of Siberia was born weighing more than 17 lb (7 kg), making her the world's heaviest baby.

Smallest Sculptures—English artist Willard Wigan creates some of the smallest sculptures on Earth. He works on rice or grains of sand and uses a surgical blade to sculpt tiny creations. You thought dwarves were small—check out the Snow White and friends above, inside the eye of a needle!

Fastest Roller Coaster

The fastest roller coaster in the world is Kinga Ka at Six Flags Great Adventure in New Jersey. At its fastest dip, it can hits speeds of 128 mph (206 km/h).

Fastest Bird—The peregrine falcon is the fastest bird in the sky and the fastest living creature. When flying, it reaches speeds of 125 mph (200 km/h). When it dives, it can glide close to 170 mph (275 km/h)!

Fastest Animal on Land— The cheetah. It can sprint at speeds of up to 60 mph (96 km/h).

WOULD YOU RATHER?

Homework or videogames? Hamburger or cabbage? Some choices in life are easy… others though require some thought.

Be a genius
or
be a millionaire.

Get paper cuts whenever you pick up paper
or
be allergic to the rain and turn bright red whenever you get wet.

Spend the rest of your life in jail, surrounded by criminals
or
spend the rest of your life in the woods, alone.

Always be really, really sweaty
or
always be really, really thirsty.

Burp fire
or
fart lightning.

Eat a gigantic spider
or
wrestle 30 rats.

Discover your next-door neighbors are vampires
or
find out your teacher is an alien.

Live in the zoo
or
live in a museum.

Walk across hot coals **or** swim across an icy river.

Be able to fly **or** be invisible.

Never have homework again **or** only have school three days a week.

Go a whole week without talking **or** go a whole year without soda.

Go a year without television **or** go a year without dessert.

Live in a world where the Sun never sets **or** live in a world where it's always dark out.

Be lost in the middle of a really, really big city **or** be trapped in a really, really small closet.

Be really, really short **or** really, really tall.

Never be able to eat your favorite food again **or** have to eat your least favorite food five times a week.

Make a ton of money doing something you hate **or** make less money doing something you love.

Smell like fish all the time **or** have a tail like a monkey.

BEST THINGS EVER SAID ABOUT
SPORTS

"There's more to **BOXING** than hitting. There's not getting hit, for instance."
GEORGE FOREMAN
BOXER

"I wanted to have **A CAREER IN SPORTS** when I was young, but I had to give it up. I'm only six feet tall, so I couldn't play basketball. I'm only 190 pounds, so I couldn't play football. And I have 20-20 vision, so I couldn't be a referee."
JAY LENO
TALK SHOW HOST

"**AWARDS** become corroded, friends gather no dust."
JESSE OWENS
ATHLETE

"**100%** **OF THE SHOTS** you don't take don't go in."
WAYNE GRETZKY
ICE-HOCKEY STAR

"I've missed more than 9,000 shots in my career. I've lost almost 300 games. 26 times, I've been trusted to take the game winning shot and missed. I've failed over and over and over again in my life. And **THAT IS WHY I SUCCEED**."
MICHAEL JORDAN
BASKETBALL PLAYER

"SUCCESS **IS NO** ACCIDENT. It is hard work, perseverance, learning, studying, sacrifice, and most of all, love of what you are doing or learning to do."

PELE
SOCCER LEGEND

"Whoever said, 'It's not whether you **WIN OR LOSE** that counts,' probably lost."

MARTINA NAVRATILOVA
TENNIS STAR

"All good athletes make **MISTAKES**; the great ones learn to make that mistake only once."

RAUL LOPEZ
BASKETBALL PLAYER

"They say that **NOBODY IS PERFECT.** Then they tell you practice makes perfect. I wish they'd make up their minds."

WILT CHAMBERLAIN
BASKETBALL STAR

"It's just a job. Grass grows, birds fly, waves pound the sand. **I BEAT PEOPLE UP.**"

MUHAMMAD ALI
BOXER

"These are **MY NEW SHOES**. They're good shoes. They won't make you rich like me, they won't make you rebound like me, they definitely won't make you handsome like me. They'll only make you have shoes."

CHARLES BARKLEY
BASKETBALL STAR

WHO AM I?

Can you figure out who I am, where I am, and what I am? Here are some clues to help. Each clue is a little easier than the last—but if you can't figure it out, the answers are on p.126.

2 I WAS BORN IN 1901.

1 I HAD A BROTHER NAMED ROY.

3 I ONCE SAID "ALL OUR DREAMS CAN COME TRUE, IF WE HAVE THE COURAGE TO PURSUE THEM."

WHERE AM I?

1 I can be seen in dozens of movies, TV shows, and video games.

3 Construction on me finished in 1889.

2 I was originally supposed to last only 20 years—but people liked me so much, they decided to let me stick around!

4 I've been visited by more than 200 million people.

WHAT AM I?

3 I AM MECHANICAL

1 NO ONE PERSON INVENTED ME—THOUGH I CAME ABOUT IN THE 18TH CENTURY.

2 ORIGINALLY, I WAS DESIGNED FOR USE BY THE BLIND.

4 I HAVE A STAR ON THE HOLLYWOOD WALK OF FAME.

6 I GAVE MY NAME TO ONE OF THE BIGGEST COMPANIES IN THE WORLD.

7 I HAVE MY OWN WORLD AND MY OWN LAND.

9 MY FAMILY NAME WAS ORIGINALLY SPELLED D'ISIGNY.

5 I RECEIVED FIFTY-NINE ACADEMY AWARD NOMINATIONS AND WON TWENTY-SIX OSCARS—THOSE ARE RECORDS!

8 WHEN YOU THINK OF ANIMATED MOVIES, YOU PROBABLY THINK OF ME.

10 I CO-CREATED MICKEY MOUSE.

5 I'm 1,063 ft (324 m) high.

8 I'm built out of 9,441 tons (8,565 tonnes) of wrought iron.

6 From the ground to the top, I have 1,710 steps.

9 I'm in Paris, France.

7 When I was first built, I was the tallest structure in the world.

6 I was designed by the engineer Gustave Eiffel.

4 I PIONEERED THE WORD "QWERTY."

7 I LED TO OTHER INVENTIONS, INCLUDING TIPP-EX.

8 PART OF MY NAME FORMS A VERB USED TODAY.

5 I HAVE OVER 40 KEYS, BUT NO LOCKS.

9 WHY USE A PEN AND PAPER?

6 MY SOUND IS USED IN THE PERCUSSION ON THE DOLLY PARTON SONG, "9 TO 5."

10 I HAVE BEEN MADE REDUNDANT BY THE DEVELOPMENT OF THE COMPUTER WORD PROCESSOR.

CHICHEN ITZA
BUILT: About 600 CE
WHERE: Mexico
WHY? This ruined city in the Mexican jungle is an astonishing example of Mayan architecture.

CHRIST THE REDEEMER
BUILT: 1931 CE
WHERE: Rio de Janeiro, Brazil
WHY? This statue of Jesus Christ in Brazil is mammoth—it stands 120 ft (38 m) tall. It is made from concrete and soapstone and weighs 700 tons (635 metric tons).

TAJ MAHAL
BUILT: About 1648 CE
WHERE: Agra, India
WHY? Emperor Shah Jahan, ruler of India's Mughal Empire, built this mausoleum in memory of his favorite wife, who died giving birth.

MACHU PICCHU
BUILT: About 1450 CE
WHERE: Peru
WHY? The "lost city of the Incas" is perched so high in the Andes Mountains that it is usually hidden in the clouds.

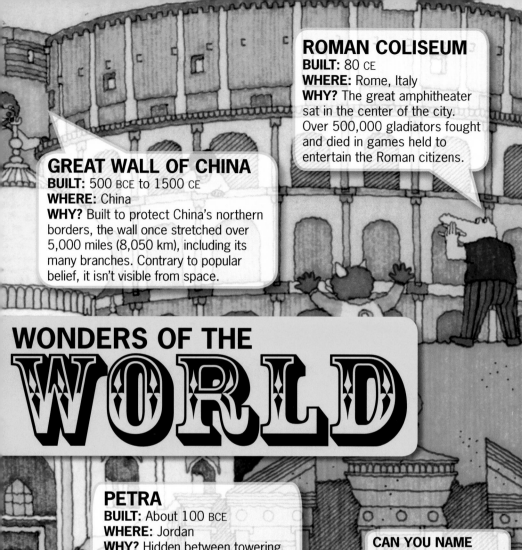

ROMAN COLISEUM
BUILT: 80 CE
WHERE: Rome, Italy
WHY? The great amphitheater sat in the center of the city. Over 500,000 gladiators fought and died in games held to entertain the Roman citizens.

GREAT WALL OF CHINA
BUILT: 500 BCE to 1500 CE
WHERE: China
WHY? Built to protect China's northern borders, the wall once stretched over 5,000 miles (8,050 km), including its many branches. Contrary to popular belief, it isn't visible from space.

WONDERS OF THE WORLD

PETRA
BUILT: About 100 BCE
WHERE: Jordan
WHY? Hidden between towering walls of rock in the Jordanian mountains are the ruins of an ancient desert kingdom. Its most majestic building, as decorative as a Greek temple, was carved out of a sheer cliff. It was a secret to the Western world until Swiss explorers found it in 1812.

CAN YOU NAME THE SEVEN WONDERS OF THE ANCIENT WORLD?
Answers on page 126

BRAINTEASERS

Feeling a little sluggish? Here are some mental puzzles to tease your brain—answers on p. 126.

HOW MANY TOYS CAN YOU FIT IN AN EMPTY BOX?

A man is trapped on an island, surrounded by water. He can't swim. Then, suddenly, one day he escapes. He uses no tools. **HOW DOES HE DO IT?**

Two women play five games of checkers. Each woman wins the same number of games. There are no ties. **HOW IS THIS POSSIBLE?**

28

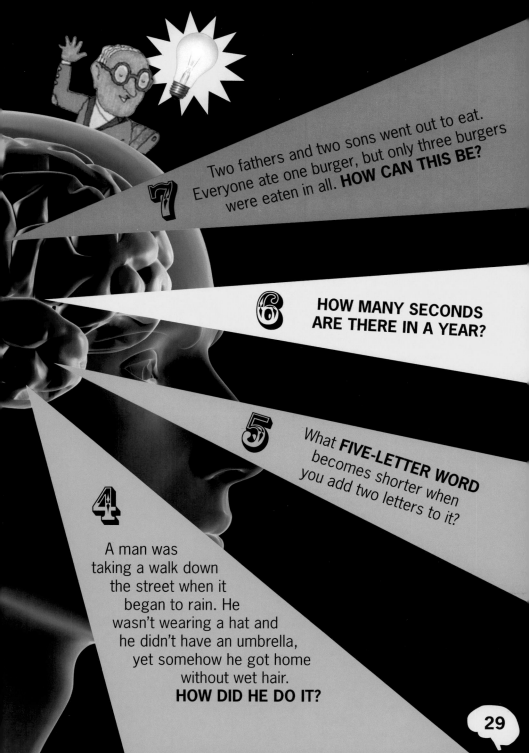

7 Two fathers and two sons went out to eat. Everyone ate one burger, but only three burgers were eaten in all. **HOW CAN THIS BE?**

6 **HOW MANY SECONDS ARE THERE IN A YEAR?**

5 What **FIVE-LETTER WORD** becomes shorter when you add two letters to it?

4 A man was taking a walk down the street when it began to rain. He wasn't wearing a hat and he didn't have an umbrella, yet somehow he got home without wet hair. **HOW DID HE DO IT?**

WEIRD NUMBERS

All those math teachers might be right:
the world is full of numbers, and here are a few
AMAZING NUMBERS that can do amazing things.

The Pirahã tribe in the Amazon only count to two—all other numbers are "many."

FORWARD AND BACK
111,111,111 × 111,111,111 = 12,345,678,987,654,321

WATCH FOR 47s!
A group known as the 47 society believes that the number 47 is the ultimate random number—they believe that it appears throughout the world more often than any other number. Give it a shot—keep your eyes peeled for the number 47. Do you think it appears more often than other numbers?

PRIME TIME
Prime numbers can only be divided by themselves or 1. The prime number 73,939,133 is a very interesting prime number—no matter how many digits you chop off the end, you still end up with a prime number. It's the largest prime known to have this property.

NUMBER WEIRDNESS

$$1 \times 8 + 1 = 9$$
$$12 \times 8 + 2 = 98$$
$$123 \times 8 + 3 = 987$$
$$1{,}234 \times 8 + 4 = 9{,}876$$
$$12{,}345 \times 8 + 5 = 98{,}765$$
$$123{,}456 \times 8 + 6 = 987{,}654$$
$$1{,}234{,}567 \times 8 + 7 = 9{,}876{,}543$$
$$12{,}345{,}678 \times 8 + 8 = 98{,}765{,}432$$
$$123{,}456{,}789 \times 8 + 9 = 987{,}654{,}321$$

UNLUCKY 13

Triskaidekaphobia is the fear of the number 13. In 1881, a group of New Yorkers formed the Thirteen Club, determined to end this phobia. On Friday the 13th, at 8:13 p.m., 13 people sat down for dinner in room 13. Nothing happened.

ALL ABOUT PI

Pi is the ratio of the circumference of a circle to its diameter. It's always the same number, whatever the size of the circle. Pi is pretty amazing because it's a never-ending number. It's usually written as **3.14**, but it can get much more precise than that. For example:
3.141592653589793238467 and on and on and on. The symbol for pi (the Greek letter "p") was first introduced by the English mathematician William Jones in 1706, who stated that π = **3.14159**. This is now the standard symbol for pi.

CALCULATOR MAGIC

- Take the number of the month you were born.
- Multiply it by 4.
- Add 13.
- Multiply by 25.
- Subtract 200.
- Add the day of the month on which you were born.
- Multiply by 2.
- Subtract 40.
- Multiply by 50.
- Add the last two digits of the year in which you were born.
- Subtract 10,500.

WHAT DO YOU GET?
RECOGNIZE THAT NUMBER?
WEIRD, HUH?

A MOUTHFUL OF FACTS

A COLLECTION OF BITE-SIZED FACTS AND STATS ABOUT TEETH AND MOUTHS. BITING STUFF!

THE AVERAGE PERSON has 32 teeth—12 molars, 8 incisors, 8 premolars, and 4 canines.

50 PERCENT OF PEOPLE say that the first thing they notice about someone is their smile—**SO BRUSH WELL!**

Back in the day, toothbrush bristles were made from the hair of cows and hogs.

Tooth enamel is the hardest thing in the human body.

AMERICANS buy 14 million gallons (53 million liters) of toothpaste every year!

A BEAVER'S TEETH never stop growing.

WEIGHING up to 12 lb (5.4 kg) each, the molars of an African elephant are as heavy as watermelons.

GIRAFFES have the same number of teeth as people: 32. But they only have front teeth on their bottom jaw. The rest are back teeth.

BIRDS don't have teeth, although they do have a bone in their tongue. Weird.

ALL SNAKES have teeth, but they don't use them for chewing. Snakes swallow their victims whole, and have backward-slanted teeth to make sure the victim doesn't slip back out.

MINNOWS (FRESHWATER FISH) have teeth in their throats.

THE DANDELION FLOWER got its name because its jagged leaf resembles a lion's tooth (*dent de lion* in French).

THE GAMES WE PLAYED

Games—you've got to love them. Kids have played games forever. Here are a few old games played way back when Grandpa was a kid.

EPHEDRISMOS

This game, played in ancient Greece, can get a bit physical. Two players put a medium-sized, but not too heavy, stone on the ground, then step back and throw other stones at it. The first player to knock over the main stone is the winner. This is where it gets fun—the winner gets to ride on the loser's back, covering the loser's eyes. The pair then run around until the losing player steps on the stone.

QUEEK

Queek was played by European children in the Middle Ages. A large, checkered cloth—like a giant, soft checkerboard—is laid out on the ground. Players then take turns calling out black or white, and then toss pebbles onto the board, trying to get their pebble to land on the color square they called out.

STOOP BALL

Popularized in New York City after World War 1, stoop ball is a street version of baseball played with a rubber ball known as a "pinkie." One player, the "batter," throws the ball at the edge of the stoop (a set of steps). The other players, the "fielders," try to catch the ball before it bounces. For every time the ball bounces before it's caught, the batter scores a point. If someone catches it, the batter is out and the person who caught it is up to bat.

HANETSUKI

This traditional Japanese game is a lot like badminton—but with no net. It's often played by girls before the new year. By tradition, the longer the girls are able to keep the shuttlecock (that's the little thing you hit back and forth) in the air, the less annoying the mosquitoes will be during the coming year.

HAWK CATCHING THE YOUNG CHICKS

Kids in China have been playing this game for hundreds of years. When the game begins, one child is chosen to be the hawk and one is chosen to be the hen. All the other kids hold hands—they're the chicks. The hawk tries to catch the chicks and the hen tries to protect them.

MAGIC

LEVITATE!

This trick is known as the Balducci levitation and it's sure to impress. It's very simple—have a friend stand about 10 ft (3 m) behind you. Turn one foot out at an angle so they can see the whole foot, but only the heel of the other. Raise the visible foot while going on to tip toes with the other foot. Do it slowly, like it takes a lot of energy to get off the ground, then drop back down quickly before your audience can figure it out. They'll be stunned!

IS THIS YOUR CARD?

This is a really simple, easy-to-do card trick. You need a normal deck of cards. Before you begin the trick, check to see what the bottom card of the deck is. For example, if it's the two of hearts, remember that. Then fan out the cards and ask a friend to "pick a card, any card, and memorize it." Have them place the card on the top of the deck and let them cut the deck. Now, simply pick up the deck and look for that two of hearts that you memorized. Whichever card is to the left of that card is your friend's card. Tah-dah!

TRICKS

COIN SWITCH

Ask a friend for a coin. Take it with your right hand and, so the audience can see, place it in the palm of your left hand. Here's the tricky part—in one quick motion, turn your hands into fists while quickly throwing the coin from your left hand to your right hand. If you do it quickly enough, the audience won't notice the toss. Now, open your hands up and show them that the coin has magically switched from one hand to the other.

MAGIC PENCIL

Here's a simple one—and all you need is a pencil. Grab your wrist with one hand and use the other hand to pick up the pencil. Then, with your "grabbing" hand, secretly extend your pointer finger and pin the pencil to the palm of your hand. Slowly open the other hand, showing only the back of the hand to the audience. To them, it'll look like the pen is magically stuck to your palm!

THINGS THEY SAY IN
HOLLYWOOD

"A celebrity is a person who works hard all his life to become well-known, then wears dark glasses to avoid being recognized."

Fred Allen (comedian)

"I know very little about acting. I'm just an incredibly gifted faker."

Robert Downey, Jr. (faker)

"Hollywood is a place where they'll pay you a thousand dollars for a kiss and fifty cents for your soul."

Marilyn Monroe (Hollywood icon)

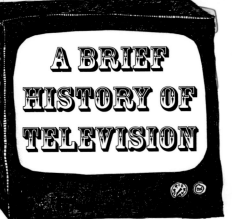

A BRIEF HISTORY OF TELEVISION

THE OLDEN DAYS

There were lots of inventions, discoveries, and experiments that resulted in the thing we now call television. But if you want to put an exact date on the beginning of TV, **it's September 1, 1928**—that's when American inventor **Philo Farnsworth** demonstrated an early version of a working electronic television.

In 1939, Farnsworth sold all of his television patents to RCA Victor for **$1 million.** The sets debuted at the **New York World's Fair** and soon after electronic televisions were available to the public. The age of TV had begun!

WHERE'S THE REMOTE?

The first wireless remote was actually for use with radios—the **Philco Mystery Control (1939)**. The first TV remote debuted in **1950**, and connected to the TV set via a wire. Its name? **The Lazy Bones**. It was cool and all, but consumers complained about tripping over the wires. So in **1955** the **Flashmatic** hit the stores—the first-ever wireless TV remote.

COLOR

CBS researchers invented the first mechanical color TV set in **1940**—but as it hit the airwaves, the quality was poor. Ten million black-and-white TVs had already been sold to the public—but just a few color sets. Ultimately, the CBS system failed, but in **1953** RCA swooped in with a better quality machine and color TV was here to stay.

CABLE TV

Although cable TV didn't become popular until the early **1990s**, it actually first started in **1948**. In towns where over-the-air reception was tough to get, **giant community antennas** were built and cables ran from them out to the individual homes. Today, **90% of American homes** have either cable or satellite TV.

HD

High-definition television (**HDTV**) hit the market in **1998**—offering sports nuts, technology lovers, and movie buffs a revolution in picture quality and sound.

THEY SAID WHAT?

"The problem with television is that the people must sit and keep their eyes glued on a screen; the average American family hasn't time for it... for this reason, if for no other, television will never be a serious competitor of broadcasting."

The New York Times, 1939

TV FIRSTS

The word "television" was first coined in 1902.
The first frozen TV dinner hit stores in 1945.
The first toilet seen on TV was in
Leave It To Beaver.
The first soap opera on TV, *War Bride*, was broadcast during the summer of 1946.
At midnight on August 1, 1981, the first music video premiered on MTV—*Video Killed the Radio Star* by the Buggles.
The Walt Disney cartoon *Donald's Cousin Gus*, was the first cartoon to appear on TV. It debuted on May 19, 1939, on NBC.

OUR POPULAR WORLD

A LOOK AT SOME OF THE THINGS PEOPLE LIKE BEST

 MOST WATCHED SPORTING EVENT

SOCCER WORLD CUP

 MOST COMMON NAME

MUHAMMAD

 MOST POPULAR ICE CREAM FLAVOR

VANILLA

 MOST COMMON LAST NAME

CHANG

 MOST POPULAR TOY

Sorry Barbie, not you this time. **IT'S LEGO!** Since everyone's famous interlocking blocks first hit the stores in 1949, over 20 billion have been made per year—that's **600 PER SECOND!**

 BEST-SELLING MUSIC ARTIST/GROUP

THE BEATLES

 MOST POPULAR SPICE

Simple old **BLACK PEPPER**

AMAZING!

 MOST POPULAR
BEVERAGE

Besides water, **IT'S TEA**. Close to **20 BILLION CUPS** of tea are drunk every day!

 MOST POPULAR
CAR COLOR

SILVER

COOL!

 MOST POPULAR
EMAIL SERVICE

YAHOO—**256.2 MILLION PEOPLE** have accounts.

 MOST POPULAR HOT
DOG TOPPING

MUSTARD

 MOST POPULAR
SPORTS TEAM

MANCHESTER UNITED

 MOST POPULAR
CANDY BAR

SNICKERS

MOST POPULAR SODA

COCA-COLA, by a landside. They sell over **683 MILLION DRINKS PER DAY!**

WOW!

 MOST VISITED
MUSEUM

THE LOUVRE—over **5 MILLION PEOPLE** visit this famous museum, home to the *Mona Lisa*, **EVERY YEAR!**

BODY LANGUAGE

So much can be given away by a LOOK or a GESTURE. Want to know what people are really saying? **Here's an insight into the body's secret code!**

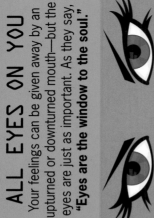

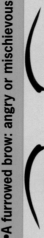

ALL EYES ON YOU

Your feelings can be given away by an upturned or downturned mouth—but the eyes are just as important. As they say, **"Eyes are the window to the soul."**

- A furrowed brow: angry or mischievous

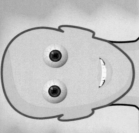
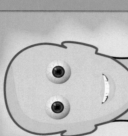

- Eyebrows raised at the center: sad

- Eyes wide open: afraid

CROSSED ARMS

One of the most basic and easily recognizable body-language signs is when someone crosses their arms across their chest. This usually means they're unconsciously **putting up a wall** around themselves—most likely because they're scared or uncomfortable. On the other hand, they could just be cold...

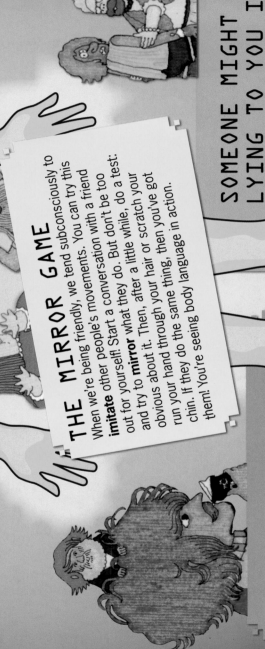

SOMEONE MIGHT BE LYING TO YOU IF:

- They avoid **eye contact** with you
- They keep touching their **face**, **mouth**, and **throat** with their hands
- They **blink** a lot
- The **timing** doesn't match between their words and gestures. For example, if someone opens a present and says "Perfect!" and then a moment later they smile—that's a lie.

THE MIRROR GAME

When we're being friendly, we tend subconsciously to imitate other people's movements. You can try this out for yourself! Start a conversation with a friend and try to **mirror** what they do. But don't be too obvious about it. Then, after a little while, do a test: run your hand through your hair or scratch your chin. If they do the same thing, then you've got them! You're seeing body language in action.

BODACIOUS BODY LANGUAGE

Some researchers think that nonverbal signals make up 80 percent of all communication. One scientist has even claimed that only seven percent of a conversation comes from spoken words. So sit up straight and make eye contact!

FOILED!
A British gang had big plans to break into a branch of the Royal Bank of Scotland. Sadly for them, they drilled into the empty office next door instead of into the bank.

SORRY, WE'RE CLOSED
Amateur criminal Christopher Allen Koch planned to rob the Pennsylvania Citizens & Northern Bank, but didn't realize it closed at noon! Employees spotted him trying to open the locked door— then gave the cops his license plate number.

BAD FIRST DATE
Bumbling, broken-hearted Brent Brown robbed an 18-year-old pizza delivery girl— then called her later and asked her out on a date! Not surprisingly, she said no. But she did give his number to the cops. They said yes… to arresting him.

7'0

6'0

5'0

4'

Some **CRIMINALS** are **INSANE** masterminds—well, that's how they are portrayed in the movies. In reality, the common crook is **JUST PLAIN STUPID…**

KARATE

One unfortunate thief attempted to break into a Colombian house, not realizing it was the home of Pan-American karate master Cristian Garces and her instructors. They spotted the burglar and proceeded to karate chop him into submission until the police arrived.

POSITIVE ID

A man from Indiana gave police officers a fake name after being pulled over. He was caught when they noticed his real name—Cecil—tattooed across his neck.

PIZZA THE ACTION

Alejandro Martinez filled out a job application at a Las Vegas pizza joint, then immediately decided to rob the place. It didn't take police long to find him—he put his real name and address on the job application!

LEFT SOMETHING BEHIND?

Another man from Indiana (what's up with the Hoosier state?) robbed a grocery store. He grabbed the money and ran—but left his wallet on the counter!

GAMES

TO PLAY IN THE CAR

"ARE WE NEARLY THERE YET?"...
You'll wish the road trip were longer with these games.

FIND FIFTY
Everyone in the car (except the driver) picks something and try to find 50 of it. For example: blue cars, flags, diners. It's a race, so first to fifty wins.

I SPY
First, pick something in the car that everyone can see. Then give a hint by saying what letter it begins with. Then everyone else gets to take a guess. Whoever guesses correctly first is the new spy and gets to pick.

TRAVEL TIP!
If you tend to get carsick, take frequent breaks from reading or playing video games and look out the window.

THE LICENSE-PLATE GAME
Spot a license plate and shout out its letters—then everyone in the car tries to come up with a **funny phrase** using those letters. If the license plate reads TGR you could say **"THIS GAME ROCKS"**!

SCAVENGER HUNT

Before you begin your trip, come up with a scavenger-hunt list. You can use one list and work together or give everybody their own list and make it a competition.

Here are a few sample things to get your hunt started:

- **Motorcycle**
- **Cemetery**
- **Police car**
- **Detour sign**
- **Car pulling a boat**

First one to spot each item on the list wins!

THE ULTIMATE CAR GAME

This is the ultimate game of the road trip universe. You'll need a pen and paper for this one. Choose a bunch of things and assign them points, e.g.:

1. **A COW = 1 POINT**
2. **AIRPLANE = 10 POINTS**
3. **CONVERTIBLE = 20 POINTS**
4. **A BOAT = 25 POINTS**
5. **HORSE TRAILER = 50 POINTS**

Keep your eyes open for **CEMETERIES**, because that's where it gets interesting. The first person to spot any cemetery gets to wipe out all the points of another player. So if you spot the cemetery, you can set your annoying brother back to zero! But be careful—whoever spots the next cemetery can wipe you out!

HISTORY'S GREATEST-EVER SCAMS & HOAXES

You've got to be kidding…? And yes they were. Here are some of the best scams and hoaxes ever. Can you believe anybody got away with them?

"IF YOU BELIEVE THAT, I HAVE A BRIDGE TO SELL YOU."

Ever heard that phrase? It means you're gullible, and it's inspired by George Parker, one of the most infamous con men in history. His scam was simple—sell famous property that he didn't own, like the Brooklyn Bridge, Grant's Tomb, the Metropolitan Museum of Art, Madison Square Garden, and even the Statue of Liberty. He was only convicted of fraud three times—even though he reportedly "sold" the Brooklyn Bridge more than twice a week! The third time's the charm though—after his third conviction in 1928, he was sent to prison for life.

NESSIE AND THE SURGEON'S PHOTO

The famous Loch Ness Monster is a creature believed to inhabit Scotland's Loch Ness. It's been the subject of many legends and hoaxes—none greater than the so-called surgeon's photo, first published in 1934. British surgeon Robert Kenneth Wilson claimed to have taken the photo of Nessie's head and neck rising out of the water. The photo was originally submitted anonymously, so it became known as simply the surgeon's photo. In 1994, the hoax was revealed—the "monster" was just a toy submarine with a head and neck made of plastic and wood.

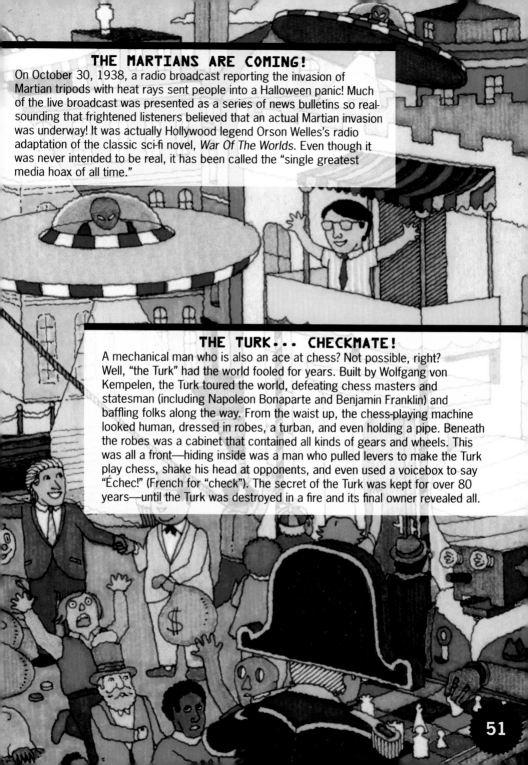

THE MARTIANS ARE COMING!

On October 30, 1938, a radio broadcast reporting the invasion of Martian tripods with heat rays sent people into a Halloween panic! Much of the live broadcast was presented as a series of news bulletins so real-sounding that frightened listeners believed that an actual Martian invasion was underway! It was actually Hollywood legend Orson Welles's radio adaptation of the classic sci-fi novel, *War Of The Worlds*. Even though it was never intended to be real, it has been called the "single greatest media hoax of all time."

THE TURK... CHECKMATE!

A mechanical man who is also an ace at chess? Not possible, right? Well, "the Turk" had the world fooled for years. Built by Wolfgang von Kempelen, the Turk toured the world, defeating chess masters and statesman (including Napoleon Bonaparte and Benjamin Franklin) and baffling folks along the way. From the waist up, the chess-playing machine looked human, dressed in robes, a turban, and even holding a pipe. Beneath the robes was a cabinet that contained all kinds of gears and wheels. This was all a front—hiding inside was a man who pulled levers to make the Turk play chess, shake his head at opponents, and even used a voicebox to say "Échec!" (French for "check"). The secret of the Turk was kept for over 80 years—until the Turk was destroyed in a fire and its final owner revealed all.

51

ANIMAL FACT-O-PEDIA

Most elephants weigh less than the tongue of a blue whale.

Polar bears are left-handed.

A group of kangaroos is called a mob.

FLAMINGOS ARE PINK BECAUSE THEY EAT SO MUCH SHRIMP.

Koalas sleep for 20 hours a day.

It's not just a tiger's fur that's striped—their skin is, too!

Pigs can get sunburned.

The Basenji is the only breed of dog that doesn't bark.

Woodpeckers can peck 20 times per second. And despite all that pecking, they never get headaches, thanks to air pockets in their skulls that cushion their (super-small) brains.

Camels have three eyelids.

A bear can run at up to 30 miles (50 km) per hour.

Cheetahs and pumas are the only big cats that don't roar—they make mewing noises like house cats.

An earthworm is like one big tongue—its body is covered in taste sensors.

Armadillos can walk underwater to cross streams and rivers.

Butterflies have taste sensors on the bottom of their feet. They taste their food by standing on it.

An ostrich's eye is bigger than its brain.

WHAT WAS built WHEN?

They may look like crumbling ruins today—but at the time these were engineering masterpieces! Here's a quick look to see who was building what, when.

3000 BCE
Stonehenge
ENGLAND

488 BCE
Parthenon
GREECE

100 BCE
Petra
JORDAN

70 CE
Roman Colosseum
ITALY

BCE

500 BCE
Persepolis
IRAN

537 CE
Hagia Sophia
Cathedral
ISTANBUL

3200 BCE
The Great
Pyramid
EGYPT

220 BCE
The Great Wall
of China
CHINA

600 CE
Chichen Itza
(Mayan civilization)
MEXICO

54

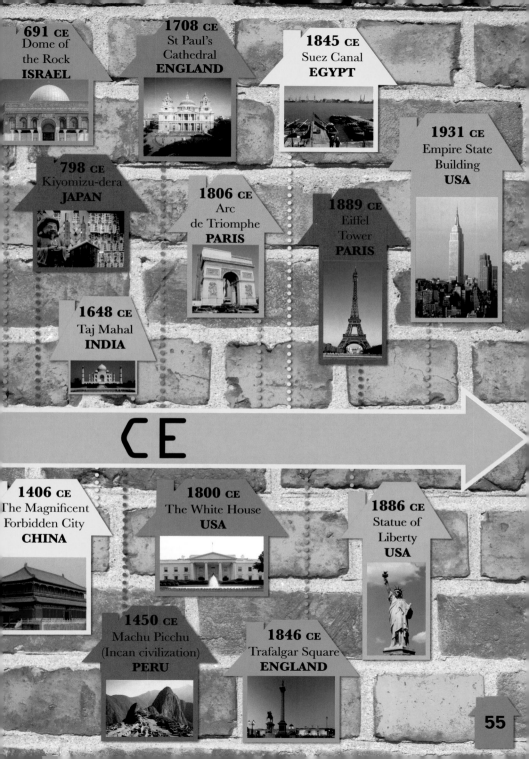

691 CE
Dome of the Rock
ISRAEL

1708 CE
St Paul's Cathedral
ENGLAND

1845 CE
Suez Canal
EGYPT

1931 CE
Empire State Building
USA

798 CE
Kiyomizu-dera
JAPAN

1806 CE
Arc de Triomphe
PARIS

1889 CE
Eiffel Tower
PARIS

1648 CE
Taj Mahal
INDIA

CE

1406 CE
The Magnificent Forbidden City
CHINA

1800 CE
The White House
USA

1886 CE
Statue of Liberty
USA

1450 CE
Machu Picchu (Incan civilization)
PERU

1846 CE
Trafalgar Square
ENGLAND

QUICK PSYCHOLOGY

Here's a quick guide to understanding psychology and some fun ways to use it in everyday life.

Subliminal messages

These are messages hidden within something else, so only your subconscious is able to see them. Here's an example: in 1957, a drive-in movie theater flashed the words **DRINK COCA-COLA** and **EAT POPCORN** for 1/3,000 of a second, every 5 seconds. They claim that they sold almost 60% more popcorn thanks to the subliminal ad.

Ivan Pavlov (1849–1936)

Pavlov was the first person to think up the idea of classical conditioning, which means learning through association. For example, if you hear the **ICE CREAM** truck, do you suddenly feel hungry? If you do, that's because you've been conditioned to associate the sound of the **ICE CREAM** truck with eating ice cream.

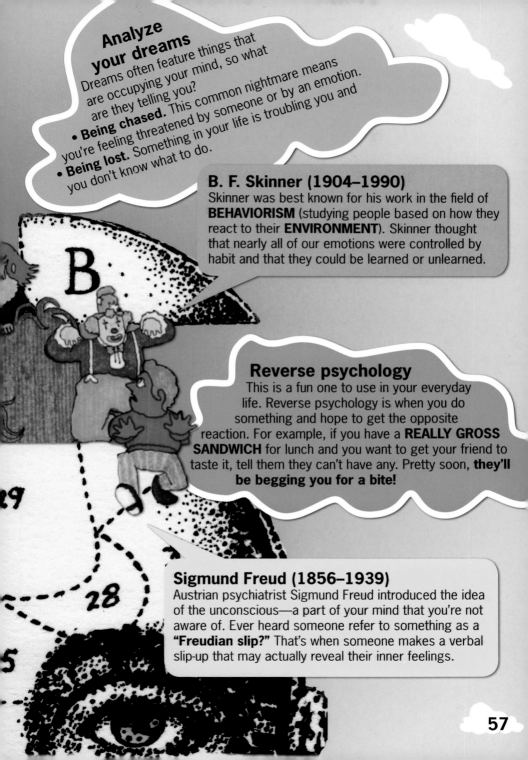

Analyze your dreams

Dreams often feature things that are occupying your mind, so what are they telling you?

- **Being chased.** This common nightmare means you're feeling threatened by someone or by an emotion.
- **Being lost.** Something in your life is troubling you and you don't know what to do.

B. F. Skinner (1904–1990)

Skinner was best known for his work in the field of **BEHAVIORISM** (studying people based on how they react to their **ENVIRONMENT**). Skinner thought that nearly all of our emotions were controlled by habit and that they could be learned or unlearned.

Reverse psychology

This is a fun one to use in your everyday life. Reverse psychology is when you do something and hope to get the opposite reaction. For example, if you have a **REALLY GROSS SANDWICH** for lunch and you want to get your friend to taste it, tell them they can't have any. Pretty soon, **they'll be begging you for a bite!**

Sigmund Freud (1856–1939)

Austrian psychiatrist Sigmund Freud introduced the idea of the unconscious—a part of your mind that you're not aware of. Ever heard someone refer to something as a **"Freudian slip?"** That's when someone makes a verbal slip-up that may actually reveal their inner feelings.

PLANETS OF THE
SOLAR SYSTEM

There are eight planets in our solar system. The inner solar system contains those planets closest to the Sun: **MERCURY, VENUS, EARTH, AND MARS.** The outer solar system contains the gas giants: **JUPITER, SATURN, URANUS,** and **NEPTUNE.**

Mercury

Mercury is similar in appearance to our Moon. It's the closest to the Sun and the smallest of the eight planets. It takes Mercury 59 days to rotate on its axis, but only 88 days to orbit the Sun—that means there are 1.49 days in a Mercury year!

Venus

Venus is small and rocky and is surrounded by thick yellow clouds. Unlike Earth clouds, which are made of water, Venus' clouds are made from poisonous sulfuric acid. The poisonous clouds reflect so much sunlight Venus shines like a star.

Earth

It's the third rock from the Sun! As far as we know right now, Earth is the only planet that supports life. The Earth's core is one of the hottest things in the universe. Earth is over 4.5 billion years old. And, oh yeah, it's where we live!

Mars

Mars, the Red Planet, is home to Olympus Mons (Latin for "Mount Olympus"), the largest mountain in the known universe. It's roughly 88,176 ft (26,875 m) high—three times as tall as Mount Everest! Mars was named after the Roman god of war.

WHAT ABOUT PLUTO?

considered to be the ninth planet. But, it's so small that recently scientists have downgraded it to a **"dwarf planet,"** making it no longer one of the official planets in our solar system.

Jupiter

Jupiter is easily the largest of the planets. It's so big that you could fit 1,000 Earths inside it! Jupiter is one of the gas giants and is made up of hydrogen and helium. It is home to the "great red spot," a violent, hundreds-of-years-old storm of swirling gas.

Saturn

Saturn is a gas giant, and is circled by thousands of bright, glowing rings. The rings are made of millions of particles ranging in size from a half an inch to a yard. Saturn has more moons than any other planet—18.

Uranus

The gas giant Uranus is made of rock and ice and colored blue by the methane in its atmosphere. Uranus is unique because it is tilted sideways. When it was visited by *Voyager 2* in 1986, its south pole was pointed at the Sun.

Neptune

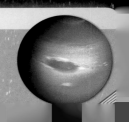

The gas planet Neptune has the fastest winds in the solar system, reaching speeds of up to 1,240 mph (2,000 km/h). Neptune was discovered in 1846 and it has still yet to make a complete orbit around the Sun! That's one long year!

SCALY!

THE WILD WORLD OF REPTILES

FIRST OF ALL—WHAT MAKES A REPTILE A REPTILE? HERE ARE THE TWO BIGGEST CLUES:

1. They're covered in scales.
2. They're cold-blooded. This doesn't mean their blood is actually cold, just that their body temperature changes with their surroundings—it takes them time to warm up!

QUESTION?

There are 8,240 species of reptiles in the world, creeping around every continent but one. Can you guess which continent?

Answers p. 126

SNAKES

• There are **3,000 TYPES OF SNAKES** in the world—but only about 40 of those are dangerous to humans. In fact, more Americans die from bee stings each year than from snakebites.

• But be careful if you're in Australia—it's the only place in the world where there are more **VENOMOUS** snakes than non-venomous snakes.

THE KING COBRA is the biggest of the baddies—this poisonous snake can grow up to 18 ft (5.5 m) in length and can weigh more than 20 lb (9 kg)!

• Look, no nose! Snakes and lizards smell by flicking their tongues into the air and capturing tiny scent particles.

SCALY!
Reptile scales are made of the same stuff as your hair.

LIZARDS

TALL AND SMALL: The largest lizard in the world is Indonesia's Komodo dragon. It can grow to 10 ft (3 m). The smallest lizard in the world is the super-small and super-rare gecko of the Virgin Islands. In fact, they're so small, only 15 of them have ever been found. Front to back, they measure ¾ in (17 mm).

TRIVIA FACTS
THINK YOUR PARENTS ARE OLD?
Some turtles live to be over a hundred and fifty years old!

CROCODILES

- **WATCH OUT!** In the water, Nile crocodiles can reach speeds of up to 29 mph (47 km/h).

- Crocodiles can't stick out their tongues. **SO THERE!**

- Crocodiles are able to grow new teeth to replace their old teeth. **NO TRIPS** to the **DENTIST**, which is probably good—what dentist would want to stick a hand in a **CROC'S MOUTH?!**

DON'T FEAR THE PHOBIA

PHOBOPHOBIA is the fear of phobias!

PHILEMAPHOBIA is the fear of kissing. And not just having to kiss your aunt Selma, but kissing anyone!

PARASKAVEDEKATRIAPHOBIA is the fear of Friday the 13th (the day and the movie).

CAN YOU GUESS WHAT THESE PHOBIAS ARE?
- **TELEPHONOPHOBIA**
- **AMNESIPHOBIA**
- **NUDOPHOBIA**
- **SOMNIPHOBIA**
- **CARNOPHOBIA**
- **BIBLIOPHOBIA**

answers p.126.

62

SCAREDY-CAT? DOES THE IDEA OF AN EIGHT-LEGGED CREEPY-CRAWLY FREAK YOU OUT? DON'T WORRY. THERE ARE WORST THINGS TO BE SCARED OF—JUST TAKE A LOOK AT THESE!

CONSECOTALEOPHOBIA is the fear of chopsticks.

COULROPHOBIA is one of the most common phobias—the fear of clowns. Johnny Depp and Daniel "Harry Potter" Radcliffe are scared of these circus comedians.

ARACHIBUTYROPHOBIA is the irrational fear of peanut butter sticking to the roof of the mouth.

ALEKTOROPHOBIA is the fear of chickens.

HIPPOPOTOMONSTROSESQUIPEDALIOPHOBIA is the fear of long words. For real. No, seriously.

ALLIUMPHOBIA is the fear of garlic. Vampires are alliumphobic, and if vampires scare you, you might be sanguivoriphobic!

63

SUPER-SLOPPY-SCIENCE
EXPERIMENTS

READY TO GET MESSY? Here are some super-fun, super-sloppy science experiments you can try at home. Make sure you have adult supervision!

SODA BOTTLE VOLCANO

WHAT YOU NEED:
- 2-liter bottle of diet soda
- Roll of Mentos candy

DO IT:
1 **OK, STEP ONE—GO OUTSIDE!** Do this one inside and your mom will hit the roof.

2 Set the bottle of soda down and carefully open it. Make sure it's somewhere that it won't fall over easily.

3 Unwrap the Mentos. This is the hard part—you want to try to drop all of the Mentos into the bottle at one time. One way to do this is to wrap tape around the Mentos, making one long stack, or drop them through a funnel.

4 Drop the Mentos into the bottle and get back! Watch the bottle volcano ERUPT!

THE SCIENCE BEHIND THE MESS
Sodas get their bubbles from the gas carbon dioxide, which is dissolved in the liquid and forms bubbles as it escapes. The rough surface of the Mentos encourages bubbles to form more quickly than usual. When you put a whole packet in, so many bubbles form that the drink turns to foam and EXPLODES.

YUCKY PUTTY

WHAT YOU NEED:

- ¼ cup cornstarch
- ¼ cup water
- mixing bowl

DO IT:

1. Pour the cornstarch into a bowl (add food coloring if you want).
2. Slowly mix the cornstarch and water together.
3. Let your new mixture stand for a couple minutes.

Now it's time to have fun. Scoop up a handful and squeeze it in your palm until it forms a hard ball. Now open your hand. The yucky putty turns back into a liquid!

THE SCIENCE BEHIND THE MESS

Yucky putty is a non-Newtonian fluid, which means that its viscosity (how runny it is) depends on how much force is applied to it. When you apply a sudden force it turns hard. When there's no force it turns liquid again. Quicksand is another non-Newtonian fluid. If you get stuck and try to escape, it becomes hard, holding you firm and trapping you!

BEST

The **BEST** things ever said about **COMPUTERS**

Joel Makower [1984]

Business analyst

"For every computer error, there are at least two human errors, one of which is blaming it on the computer."

Ken Olsen [1977]

President of Digital Equipment Corporation

"There is no reason for any individual to have a computer in their home."

Pablo Picasso [1881–1973]

Painter

"Computers are useless. They can only give you answers."

Grace Murray Hopper [1945]

On the removal of a two-inch-long moth from an experimental computer at Harvard:

"From then on, when anything went wrong with a computer, we said it had bugs in it."

Winn Schwartau [1994]

Computer expert

"Software is what makes your computer behave and look smarter than it is."

Mr. Azae [1957]

Television executive to computer designer Richard Sumner in the great Spencer Tracy/ Katharine Hepburn movie *Desk Set*:

"I don't understand a word you're saying, but it sounds great."

David D. Thornburg [1985]

Writer

"Who has such a large Christmas card mailing list that you need to keep it on a computer? If so, why aren't I on it?"

Gene DeWeese [1984]

Sci-fi author

"The first digital computer, of course, was a set of 10 fingers that somebody realized could be used for counting."

Thomas J. Watson [1943]

Chairman of IBM

"I think there is a world market for about five computers."

Bruce Knapp [1984]

Commenting on the role of supercomputers:

"It means you can try to answer questions you thought the universe was going to do without."

101 cures for BOREDOM

Bored? Bored of being bored? Here are 101 ways to escape the boring prison of King Bore and his Boredomian Army.

1. Search for belly button lint.
2. Draw your family tree—see how many generations back you can go.
3. Learn to whistle.
4. Make shadow puppets.
5. Write a short story.
6. Read a short story.
7. Write a rap about your short story.
8. Do stuff—throw, write, brush your teeth with your "other" hand.
9. Prepare and serve a three-course dinner.
10. Plant some seeds.
11. Teach yourself to burp on command.
12. Write your memoirs in rhyme.
13. Count the number of hairs in one square inch of your arm.
14. Write a note to the leader of your country.
15. Make a list of 20 things that make you angry.
16. Now, make a list of 20 things that make you happy.
17. Make a list of 20 things you are proud of.
18. Make a list of 20 things you want to change about yourself..
19. Count 1,000 somethings—like trees, pebbles, coins, ideas, people, or leaves.
20. Make a list of the top 10 things you want to do in your life.
21. Write an original joke.
22. Learn your favorite poem.
23. Come up with your own 101 somethings, write them down, and send them to this book's publisher for possible inclusion in the next edition.
24. Think of a cool new nickname for yourself.
25. Play a game of solitaire.
26. Skip a stone.
27. Juggle (Can't? Turn to p. 72).
28. Toss a ball in the air and catch it. How many times can you catch it without dropping?
29. Write a song.
30. Draw your dream house.
31. Memorize a famous speech.
32. Invent a sandwich.
33. Make a house of cards.
34. Clean up your room.
35. Learn to tie a new knot.
36. Make a movie.
37. Build a fort.
38. Start keeping a journal.
39. Twiddle your thumbs.
40. Watch a funny video on YouTube.
41. Measure how far you can spit.
42. Learn the alphabet backward.
43. Draw yourself in the mirror.
44. Take photos.
45. Learn how to cook a fun and easy meal.
46. Rearrange your bedroom.
47. Learn about the history of where you live.
48. Make breakfast in bed for your parents.
49. Learn to do a headstand, cartwheel, and somersault.
50. Create a costume out of your clothes.
51. Draw the view from your bedroom window.

52 · Take a bath.

53 · Talk to yourself.

54 · Make up a secret handshake.

55 · Try out a new hairstyle.

56 · Exercise.

57 · Make an art project—like a collage.

58 · Decorate a T-shirt.

59 · Tell all your friends about this amazing new book you're reading (y'know, this book in your hands!).

60 · Learn the definition of a new word and use it in a sentence.

61 · Draw a floor plan for an awesome tree house.

62 · Cut out black-and-white pictures from magazines and color them in.

63 · Write a poem.

64 · Flip a coin 10 times, 50 times, 100 times—what comes up more often?

65 · Rename the constellations—they are VERY out of date.

66 · Invent a superhero with a completely original power.

67 · Learn the alphabet in French, or Spanish, or Greek, or all three.

68 · Invent a word.

69 · Invent a word that perfectly describes your mood or feelings right now.

70 · Invent a word that describes you perfectly.

71 · Invent a word that sounds like what the word means—like BANG or POP.

72 · Design a calling or business card for yourself.

73 · Imagine yourself at 70 years old. Now write a biography of your life.

74 · Figure out the five best places to hide money, should anybody ever break into your home.

75 · Then go check out those five places; see if anyone ever hid any money there and then forgot about it.

76 · Invent a coded written language.

77 · Invent a spoken secret language and start using it with best friends.

78 · Invent a club. Who would be in it? Now, write its charter.

79 · Write a letter to yourself, put it away, and open it in 10 years.

80 · Make a paper airplane. Make two, and race them.

81 · Turn all the lights off and pretend you're camping in a wild jungle.

82 · Make a basketball hoop out of a trash can. See how far away you can stand and still make a shot.

83 · Make ice cube popsicles out of juice or soda.

84 · Make a sock-puppet hero and a sock-puppet monster. Have them do battle.

85 · Make a telephone out of two cups and some string.

86 · Create a stand-up comedy routine. Perform it for your parents.

87 · Blow up a balloon and play volleyball with a friend.

88 · Make up an imaginary friend.

89 · Come up with the ultimate candy bar. What would be in it? What would you call it?

90 · Climb a tree.

91 · Design and make a new game.

92 · Create a new dance.

93 · Get a BIG piece of paper and try to trace your entire body.

94 · Measure the amount of steps from one place to another. For example, how many steps does it take to get from your bedroom to outside and back again?

95 · Play connect the dots with the moles and freckles on your arms. Don't use permanent markers!

96 · Choreograph a movie-style sword fight.

97 · Play any sport—but use a Frisbee instead!

98 · Find a mirror. Make the weirdest face possible. Go show someone.

99 · Watch TV on mute and make up new dialog for the characters.

100 · Try a new food.

101 · Call someone just to talk.

OPTICAL ILLUSIONS

These visual enigmas play tricks with your mind by confusing the way you see shapes and movement.

PENROSE TRIANGLE

At first glance this shape may look real, but look again—those angles are completely impossible!

MOVING IMAGE ILLUSIONS

These two pictures aren't really moving—are they? The patterns confuse your brain into **thinking** it sees movement just out of your focus, no matter where you look.

FALSE SPIRAL ILLUSION

Try tracing your finger around a curve of this "spiraling" shape, and you'll find that it's not a spiral at all, but a series of rings.

3-D ILLUSIONS

Both of these images use flat shapes to create an illusion of depth. 3-D boxes pop out at you from the picture on the right—but are the yellow shapes the tops of the cubes, or the bottoms?

HOW TO

The best place to start if you want to be a clown is to learn to juggle. EASY! Well, let's see.

GETTING STARTED

First things first! You are going to need three juggling balls. Or three socks rolled into balls.

So you've got your three balls, now drop two. Get used to it—you'll be dropping a lot as you learn. Now, with your one ball, you are ready to start.

WHERE TO LEARN

The best place to learn is outside. Why? There's more space out there, and trust me, you are going to need it.

1. ONE-BALL ARCS

This is the most important skill to master. It is the foundation of the whole juggling technique. Make sure you are stood comfortably, and throw the ball from your right hand to your left hand in a smooth arc. The ball should peak at eye-level. Now throw it back from left hand to right. Keep this up until you can confidently and consistently arc the ball from right to left and back again.

JUGGLE

2. TWO-BALL SWITCH

You have now perfected the one-ball arc. Now, pick up a second ball. This part of the learning process is about timing. Stand comfortably with one ball in each hand. Make sure there is plenty of space around you. Throw the right-hand ball, as it reaches the top of the arc, throw the left-hand ball inside the arc of the first ball. Continue until you can throw and catch both balls.

3. THREE-BALL CYCLE

You can now throw and catch two balls. The next step is—you guessed it—the third ball. This step is all about rhythm. Hold two balls in your right hand, and one in your left. Perform the two-ball switch, and as the second ball reaches eye-level, throw the third ball (again, inside the arc.) You will definitely start to move about as you try to master this, so remember to practice outside.

4. FOREVER JUGGLING

With the three-ball cycle mastered, you are nearly there. All that is left to do is to keep going. As you toss the third ball and it reaches the peak of its arc, throw ball number one, and start the cycle again. With a lot of practice, patience, and concentration you could juggle forever...

SUPER -LAME SUPER- HEROES

Everyone knows about Superman, Spiderman, and the Joker. But what about those less popular comic book characters who gathered dust in attics and garages? Here we present some of the less fortunate, more obscure, and least successful superheroes.

MATTER-EATER LAD

Matter-Eater Lad is a member of the Legion of Super-Heroes. He has the ability to eat anything. Absolutely anything! The Legion of Super-Heroes has actually employed a number of pretty lame superheroes over the years, including Bouncing Boy (he can bounce), Chlorophyll Kid (has the ability to make plants grow extra fast), and Infectious Lass (see across the page).

ZAN FROM THE WONDER TWINS

Zan had one of the most useless powers ever—the ability to turn into ice, water, or steam. And worst of all, his twin sister, Zayna, had an awesome power— she could turn into any animal, even a mythological one. So, while Zan's stuck transforming into an ice cube, his sister can fly around as a griffin. Not fair.

MADAM FATAL
Despite the name, Madam Fatal was actually a man. Retired actor Richard Stanton dressed up as a little old lady and fought crime using his natural athleticism and supreme fighting skills. He used the little old lady get-up to catch villains off guard.

KITE MAN
This obscure Batman villain didn't really have any superpowers—he was just really, really good at hang-gliding. He was also armed with a whole bunch of kite-related weapons. Sadly, Kite Man is no longer with us—he was killed by Bruno Mannheim, a much-cooler supervillain.

BROTHER POWER THE GEEK
This 60s superhero was a mannequin that was struck by lightning, bringing him to life and giving him pretty much unlimited magical powers. He used his superpowers to… become a politician and run for Congress! Everyone realized how lame he was right away—he lasted all of two issues.

INFECTIOUS LASS
This DC comics superhero has the ability to give anyone a sickness or disease (only temporarily, though). So, say, the Joker's about to rob a bank—she could give him the flu. Gotcha... Atchoo!

75

WHY IS THE
SKY BLUE?

Some things in life we take for granted. Grass is green, and the sky is blue—but why? Here are a few answers to questions you may have wondered about.

Why does the wind blow?

When the Sun heats Earth, it also heats Earth's atmosphere. As the air gets warmer, it rises, and cold air moves in and replaces the hot air. That air movement is wind blowing!

Why do we have eyebrows?

Two reasons. Eyebrows keep sweat from running off the forehead and into the eyes, which can make it really hard to see. Also, they allow people to make facial expressions that other people can understand.

Why are mosquito bites soooo itchy?

Mosquitoes bite you so they can suck up your blood. But in order to keep your blood from clotting and drying up, they inject you with a little saliva when they bite. It's the chemicals in that saliva that make you so itchy.

Why is the sky blue?

Sunlight is made up of all the colors of the rainbow. As it travels toward us through Earth's atmosphere, it runs into trillions of tiny air molecules. Most of the different colors pass straight through the air, but blue light bounces off in a new direction when it strikes an air molecule. As a result, this light gets scattered right across the sky, making it look blue!

How are spiders able to walk up walls?

There are two different reasons. Some spiders have microscopic hairs on their feet that grasp the bumps and grooves in walls and ceilings. Other spiders daub their feet with the sticky silk that they use to make webs so they can cling to surfaces.

Why do leaves fall off trees as the weather changes?

Leaves harness the Sun's energy to make food so that trees can grow. But to do this they need lots of water. In winter, when the ground freezes, trees can't get enough water for the leaves, and there isn't much sunlight anyway. So trees with large, tender leaves let them die and fall off and then grow new ones in spring.

EVERYBODY'S WONDERED ABOUT WHAT LIFE WOULD BE LIKE ON ANOTHER PLANET. But could humans actually go out and colonize another planet? Right now, no one knows for sure, but it's definitely a possibility.

Similarities to Earth

Recent unmanned missions to Mars have revealed the presence of water ice on Mars. So it appears the Red Planet has all the necessary elements to support life.

Unlike some planets in our solar system, Mars has an atmosphere. It's super-thin (roughly 1% of Earth's atmosphere), but it's strong enough to provide protection from the Sun's radiation.

The Martian day (known as a sol) is very close to Earth's—24 hours and 39 minutes.

Mars has seasons like Earth, but they are twice as long because the Martian year is 669 sols.

NOW, WITH THAT SAID— THERE ARE STILL A LOT OF DIFFERENCES BETWEEN EARTH AND MARS THAT WILL MAKE COLONIZATION DIFFICULT.

MARS

Differences from Earth

The surface gravity on Mars is about ⅓ that of Earth's. That's awesome because you can kick a ball about a mile—but, there are also health problems that go along with that level of weightlessness.

The Martian atmosphere contains the right gases, but in different amounts. Earth's atmosphere contains 78% nitrogen, 21% oxygen, and 0.038% carbon dioxide. Mars is mainly carbon dioxide—95%—with 2.7% nitrogen and only 0.13% oxygen.

Mars is way too cold—as in Antarctica cold. Brrr.

There are no large bodies of liquid water on Mars' surface—¾ of Earth's surface is covered by water.

TO MAKE MARS HABITABLE, WE NEED TO DO TWO MAJOR THINGS: ALTER THE ATMOSPHERE AND ADD HEAT.

So here's one crazy way to make MARS livable for humans—change it! **Terraforming**, which literally means "Earth-shaping," is the hypothetical process of changing a planet's temperature, atmosphere, ecology, and surface, to make it habitable for us human folk.

10 THINGS TO DO WITH A...
SPARE TIRE

Car tires can take thousands of years to decompose, so rather than throw them away—recycle! Here are ten things to do with a spare tire.

MAKE A SANDBOX

FIND LOTS AND MAKE A HOUSE

MAKE A TIRE SWING

THROW A BALL THROUGH IT

GET TWO TIRES AND RACE THEM

STACK A FEW AND BUILD A FORT

FILL WITH WATER AND MAKE A MINI POND

USE IT AS A CHAIR FOR YOUR TREE HOUSE

SPLASH SOME PAINT ON IT—MODERN ART!

SHRED IT UP AND USE IT AS BOUNCY ARTIFICAL TURF

TRASH OR TREASURE ?

10 THINGS TO DO WITH AN OLD SOCK

1. Make a sock puppet.
2. Make an entire sock puppet family and put on a show!
3. Cut off the end and make a cool wrist band or arm band. Decorate it!
4. Secret safe! Hide stuff in it and stick it in your drawer—no one will ever think to look in there.
5. Stick a tennis ball inside it, tie it up, and make a great pet toy.
6. Put your hand in it and use it to dust your bedroom, your computer monitor, your TV—anything!
7. Cut four holes in it—Hamster outfit.
8. Stuff it with beans and you've got a hacky sack.
9. Sunglasses case.
10 Find three, roll them up—juggling balls!

10 THINGS TO DO WITH AN EMPTY PLASTIC BOTTLE

1. Get 10 of them and go bowling.
2. Ring toss!
3. Draw a little door on it, fill it with action figures, and you've got a bathtub submarine!
4. Decorate it and make a pencil holder.
5. Fill it with pebbles and make a little musical instrument.
6. Make a flower pot and give it to your mom as a gift.
7. Fill with something heavy and make a door stop.
8. Perfect piggy bank.
9. Gather all those sock puppets you made and play spin the bottle.
10. Perfect for filling water balloons in the midst of a water fight!

BEST THINGS EVER SAID BY CARTOON CHARACTERS

Cartoon characters look funny, have funny voices, and say the funniest things…

Porky Pig: **"TELL ME, MR. HOLMES, WHERE DID YOU GO TO SCHOOL TO LEARN TO BE A DETECTIVE?"**

"I'LL RISE, BUT I WON'T SHINE."

Garfield the cat

Daffy Duck: **"ELEMENTARY, MY DEAR WATKINS. ELEMENTARY."**

Looney Tunes

"I DON'T KNOW! I DON'T KNOW WHY I DID IT, I DON'T KNOW WHY I ENJOYED IT, AND I DON'T KNOW WHY I'LL DO IT AGAIN!"

Bart Simpson, *The Simpsons*

"IF IT WASN'T FOR BAD LUCK, I'D HAVE NO LUCK AT ALL."

George Jetson, The Jetsons

"YABBA DABBA DOO!"

Fred Flintstone, *The Flintstones*

That's a job?

When I grow up I want to be a smell checker...

Yep, there is such a job! Don't feel like you have to restrict yourself to being a doctor, lawyer, or astronaut! Check out these crazy vocations.

PLEASE DON'T MIS THIS TIME!!

Knife thrower's assistant
Okay, this one definitely wins the award for scariest. But it's real. Professional knife throwers need someone to act as human targets in their stage acts. And if you've got the guts, that someone could be you!

HE STINKS!

Smell checker
Like having your head in armpits all day? Then this could be the job for you. It's the responsibility of some laboratory researchers to do smell checks to make sure that antiperspirants and deodorants are actually doing their job. Hmmm...

Fruit colorer

Fruit is often picked before it's ripe, so that by the time it gets to your supermarket, it's just hitting its peak. To make the fruit look good, a colorer sprays it with chemicals to make it look appetizing. Beware of any fruit stamped "color added."

Roller-coaster engineer

Now here's an awesome job. Teams of roller-coaster engineers design every part of a roller coaster—the loops, the drops, and the track—but you'll need to get a degree in engineering. School many not be fun, but it's worth it to get to ride the roller coasters first!

Master sniffer

George Aldrich is NASA's official "master sniffer." He has a staff of 25 people who smell everything that goes on a space shuttle. Things act differently in space, and no astronaut wants to be stuck with an awful odor—you can't open a window to get fresh air.

Dog food tester

Simon Allison is a senior food technologist—who eats pet food for a living. Just like any other food, pet food needs to be tested. So, how does it taste? It's quite bland, really," Simon says. "Dogs enjoy all foods, while cats are more choosy."

Circus elephant tender

Like elephants? Like the circus? Like HUGE piles of poop? If so, we've found your dream job. Elephant tenders take care of the animals behind the scenes—and that involves shoveling a lot of elephant doo-doo. Not only is it gross, but one elephant foot on your head, and you're a pancake.

HOW MUCH POOP??

PIRATE-O-PEDIA

What exactly makes a pirate a pirate? Just dressing up in a goofy outfit, not showering, and carrying a sword isn't enough. Real-life pirates were rough and tough types who traveled the high seas and plundered ships for gold, weapons, and other valuables. So, are you a sea dog or a landlubber?

FAMOUS FICTIONAL PIRATE
Long John Silver—The villain of Robert Louis Stephenson's novel *Treasure Island*, Long John is the inspiration for much of today's pirate lore—he had a parrot, a peg leg, and walked using a crutch.

Dead Man's Chest isn't actually a chest—it's an island in the Caribbean Sea. Legend has it that Blackbeard stranded 15 of his crew there as punishment for mutiny.

FAMOUS FICTIONAL PIRATE
Captain Hook—Peter Pan's nemesis Captain Hook lost his hand to a hungry crocodile. While some real pirates had hooks, Captain Hook is responsible for the popular image of the hook-handed pirate.

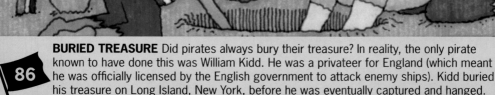

BURIED TREASURE Did pirates always bury their treasure? In reality, the only pirate known to have done this was William Kidd. He was a privateer for England (which meant he was officially licensed by the English government to attack enemy ships). Kidd buried his treasure on Long Island, New York, before he was eventually captured and hanged.

FAMOUS REAL PIRATE
Anne Bonny—Female pirates were rare, and Anne Bonny was the most infamous of all of them. She was eventually captured and sentenced to execution, but then she completely disappeared! Some say she spent the rest of her life as a housewife.

The Jolly Roger
The official pirate flag was the Jolly Roger. It was a black flag with a white skull and crossbones. Sound scary? Well it was supposed to be...

Piece of eight
This is a Spanish one-ounce silver coin. It was roughly equivalent to one US dollar.

Why are pirates so mean? Because they Arrrrrr!

FAMOUS REAL PIRATE
Blackbeard—The vicious captain of the *Queen Anne's Revenge*, Blackbeard is probably the most famous of the real-life pirates. According to legend, he once shot his first mate because "if he didn't shoot one or two crewmen now and then, they'd forget who he was." Oh, and he had a black beard.

SUPERBUGS

People who study bugs are **"ENTOMOLOGISTS."**

Termites have **BACTERIA** in their stomachs to help them digest wood. Because these little stomach creatures produce a lot of methane, termites **FART** like crazy.

A **QUEEN ANT** can lay **30,000** eggs a month for up to 10 years.

ANTS CAN LIVE FOR 16 YEARS.

If you put **40 FIREFLIES** in a glass jar, you should be able to read by the **LIGHT THEY GIVE OFF.**

Fleas jump **130 TIMES** their own height. That's like a **PERSON JUMPING** over a 65-story building.

If ants were **HUMAN SIZED**, they could run five times as fast as a record-breaking **OLYMPIC** runner.

BUTTERFLIES HAVE 12,000 EYES.

The tiny silver eggs that mother lice stick to the hairs on a **LICE-INFECTED** head are called "nits." Nits often have to be removed by picking through each strand of hair. Thus, the term **"NITPICKY"** for people who are very fussy.

Say this **10 TIMES**, fast: "Moths munch mushy mushrooms."

Some tarantulas can go two years without eating.

Some people consider chocolate ants a delicacy.

Mosquitoes flap their wings 1,000 times per second.

The world's **SMALLEST SPIDER** is half the size of this **PERIOD.**

ONLY FEMALE MOSQUITOES BITE YOU.

HORNETS EAT HOUSEFLIES. Some American settlers used to hang hornets' nests in their homes to get rid of flies.

BEES are more likely to sting people on **WINDY DAYS** than in any other kind of weather.

Ghost stories

What's your favorite scary story? Here are some to share around a roaring fire, in the dead of night, on Halloween…

MIDNIGHT RIDE

It was a cloudly, moonless night. A young man named Ryan was driving home when he passed a pretty young girl waiting by the side of the road. Being a nice guy, he pulled over and asked the girl if she needed a ride home. It was starting to rain and a chill was creeping through the air, so Ryan gave the girl his jacket to keep warm. Ryan asked the girl for her name. She was silent for a moment, then said it was Christina. They drove through the rain for an hour before they got to her house. Christina thanked Ryan for the ride, and he drove back home.

The next morning he realized that he had left his jacket with Christina. He drove back to Christina's house, but when he knocked on the door, an old woman answered. Ryan asked for Christina. The old woman said nothing, then angrily tried to slam the door in his face. That's when Ryan noticed a photo of Christina sitting on the mantel. "That's her!" Ryan said, pointing at the photo. The old woman's face turned white. "What is it?" Ryan asked.

The old woman told Ryan that her daughter had been dead for 15 years. In fact, she died 15 years ago, last night. Ryan couldn't believe it. "No, I need to see her grave," he said. Ryan got in his car and raced to the cemetery. Just steps inside, he saw a grave with the name Christina on it. And there, sitting on top of the gravestone, was his jacket.

My dearest Christina
R.I.P.

THE RMS *QUEEN MARY*

Could the *RMS Queen Mary I* really be haunted? Like, for real, real-life haunted? Many people think so and some even claim to have seen the ghosts themselves!

The *RMS Queen Mary I* is a retired ocean liner that sailed the North Atlantic Ocean from 1936 to 1967. During World War II she shuttled thousands of troops across the Atlantic. During the war, she was painted all gray to camouflage her on the high seas and she was known as the "Gray Ghost."

During her 60-year sailing history, 59 people died on board and some of them still haunt the ship today. The pool area is the most haunted part of the ship. According to legend, a young girl tried to slide down the banister of the pool stairs, but a wave tossed her aside and she broke her neck when she fell. Her ghost now wanders the pool area, looking for her mother.

Crewman John Pedder was crushed by a huge steel door during an evacuation drill. Banging can often be heard coming from behind the door, and his ghost, clad in the blood-soaked blue coveralls in which he died, is often seen wandering the corridor to the engine room. That's not all. Many people have reported hearing the sounds of crying children coming from what was once the playroom.

So, could the ship really be haunted? The only way to know for sure is to go visit the ship yourself. She's docked in California and you can take a tour.

Or are you too scared?

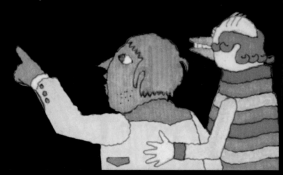

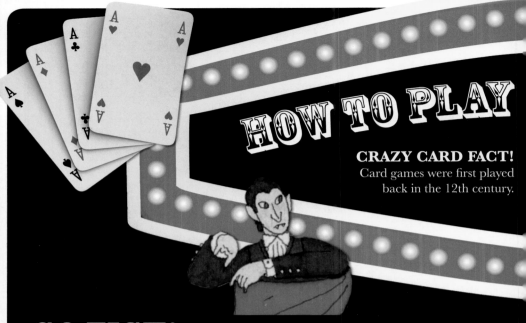

CRAZY CARD FACT!
Card games were first played back in the 12th century.

GO FISH! (2 TO 6 PLAYERS)

1 Deal each player seven cards (unless you have more than four players, then deal each player five cards.)

2 Throw the rest of the cards into the middle of the table. This is the "fish pond"—the pool of cards you will be taking from throughout the rest of the game.

3 Choose a player to go first. Go by youngest, oldest, smelliest—up to you.

4 The goal of Go Fish is to collect the most sets of four—for example, four kings, four tens, or four fours.

5 Whoever goes first—let's say it's you—can ask any other player for any card. For example, say you want a Jack. If the player you ask has that card, he/she must give it to you. Then you get to go again.

6 If not, he/she says **"Go Fish!"** and you then take a card from the fish pond. If you get the card you wanted, show everyone, and go again. If not, keep your card, and the player to your left gets a turn.

7 Whenever you get a group of four card, place it on the table in front of you. When the fish pond is empty, count up your foursomes. Whoever has the most, wins.

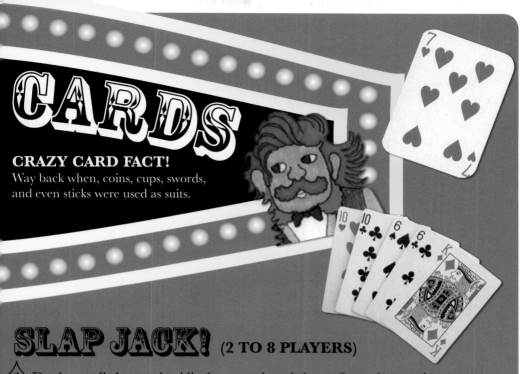

CARDS

CRAZY CARD FACT!
Way back when, coins, cups, swords, and even sticks were used as suits.

SLAP JACK! (2 TO 8 PLAYERS)

1 Deal out all the cards. All players should put their cards in a stack, face down, so they can draw from them without looking.

2 The player to the left of the dealer goes first by taking the top card from his/her pile and tossing it face up in the middle of the table. When tossing a card, make sure you turn the card away from yourself so you don't see it before the other players. Do it quickly, so no one has an advantage.

3 Play continues to the left until a Jack is thrown, then it's time to **Slap Jack!** Every player tries to slap the Jack. Whoever gets his/her

hand down first wins, and gets to take all the cards in the pile.

4 Continue playing. Each time a Jack is slapped the winner takes the pile. When players run out of cards from their original piles, they can use the cards won from the Slap Jack pile.

5 If you run out of cards and don't have a pile, then you're out. The game keeps going until one person has the entire deck.

6 Want to make the game a little more slappy? Don't just slap the Jacks, slap any picture card—Kings, Queens, even Aces.

THE INTERNET

A BRIEF HISTORY OF THE INTERNET

THE INTERNET STARTED IN THE LATE 1960S and early 1970s, when the United States Defense Department began researching ways to allow networks of computers to communicate with one another. The idea was to link government and university research centers and share information. As time passed, the network grew and grew, until it included businesses, schools, companies, and regular people like you and me. Today, over one-and-a-half billion people across the world are connected and interacting every day...

ALL VIA THE INTERNET!

INTERNET VIRUSES are programs or pieces of code that sneak onto your computer and then mess it up. Some are just annoying, causing programs to crash, but others can completely destroy a computer.

CHAT ROOM SHORT HAND

BRB =	be right back
BTW =	by the way
IMHO =	in my humble opinion
KK =	OK
BFF =	best friends forever
LOL =	laughing out loud
OTOH =	on the other hand
TTYL =	talk to you later
ROFL =	rolling on the floor laughing

WATCH OUT FOR EMAIL VIRUSES

EVERYTHING YOU EVER WANTED TO KNOW ABOUT THE INTERNET AND THE
WORLD WIDE WEB.

THE INTERNET VS. THE WORLD WIDE WEB

Despite what you might think—the Internet and the World Wide Web aren't the same thing. The **World Wide Web** is the system we use to access the Internet through browsers like Firefox and Internet Explorer. Think of it like this—the **Internet** is a **country** and the **World Wide Web** is the **capital**. Although, if it were up to us, we'd name it **Webville…or Webtown!**

INTERNET FACTS

- **1 billion** users around the globe surf the Internet every month.
- There are more than **8 billion** Internet pages, and counting!
- **80% of online shoppers are WOMEN.**
- One of the most amazing things about the Internet is that it's **not owned by any country, company, or corporation.**
- The Internet is growing super fast! It took only **5 years** for the Internet to reach **5 million users**. It took **38 years for radio to reach 5 million users and 13 years for TV!**
- Internet search company **Google** gets its name from the word **Googol**, which represents the number 10,000,000,000,000,000,000,000,000,000,000,000,000,000,000,000,000,000,000,000,000,000,000,000,000,000,000,000,000,000,000,000.
- In Iceland, **86%** of people are online.

FAMOUSLY WRONG PREDICTIONS

"Half of the people can be part right all of the time.
Some of the people can be all right part of the time.
But all people can't be right all of the time…"
Bob Dylan, singer/songwriter.

WISE WORDS… AND ALL THESE PEOPLE WERE TOTALLY WRONG!!!!

"We don't like their sound, and guitar music is on the way out." Decca Recording Co. while rejecting the Beatles (1962).

"I think there is a world market for maybe five computers." Thomas Watson, chairman of IBM (1943).

"This telephone has too many shortcomings to be seriously considered as a means of communication. The device is inherently of no value to us." Western Union internal memo (1876).

"Heavier-than-air flying machines are impossible." Lord Kelvin, British physicist, inventor, and president of the Royal Society (1895).

"You'd better learn secretarial work or else get married." Emmeline Snively, Director, Blue Book Modeling Agency, to Norma Jean Mortenson (Marilyn Monroe).

D'OH!

"People will soon get tired of staring at a plywood box every night."
Darryl F. Zanuck, on television (1946).

NO WAY!

"A rocket will never be able to leave the Earth's atmosphere."
New York Times (1936).

"The horse is here to stay, but the automobile is only a novelty—a fad."
Michigan Savings Bank president's advice to Henry Ford's lawyer on why not to invest in Ford Motor Company.

"Airplanes are interesting toys but of no military value."
Marechal Ferdinand Foch, Professor of Strategy, Ecole Superieure de Guerre, France.

"Nuclear-powered vacuum cleaners will probably be a reality in 10 years."
Alexander Lewyt, President, Lewyt Corp. (1953).

"Space travel is utter bilge."
Richard van der Riet Wooley, British Astronomer Royal (1956).

"Everything that can be invented has been invented."
Charles H. Duell, Commissioner, US Office of Patents (1899).

"Rail travel at high speed is not possible because passengers, unable to breathe, would die of asphyxia."
Dr Dionysys Larder (1793–1859).

SILLY!

ALIENS and UFOS

Little green men from Mars? Or scary, hairy Klingons from… Klingon? Are aliens just something out of science fiction, or is there really something out there?

WHY SAUCERS?

UFOs are usually imagined as flying saucers. But why? It all started with pilot Kenneth A. Arnold, the first American to report a UFO. He was flying a plane over Washington State in 1947, when he saw nine objects that he said looked "flat like a pie-pan and somewhat bat-shaped." Newspaper articles began referring to the UFOs as flying saucers—whether it was Arnold who first used the term "flying saucers" or a reporter is still a mystery.

FACTS

Every three minutes a UFO sighting occurs somewhere on the planet.

A 1991 survey stated that 4 million Americans believe they have been abducted by aliens. That's as many as the whole population of Puerto Rico!

IF THERE ARE ALIENS, WHY WON'T THE GOVERNMENT JUST TELL US?

You might be wondering—if aliens have landed on Earth, why keep it a big secret? In 1961, NASA submitted a report called the "Proposed Studies on the Implications of Peaceful Space Activities for Human Affairs." It claimed that, if people were confronted with beings from another planet, we would probably freak out. Who wouldn't?

Close Encounters of the Third Kind is a classic UFO movie. But what's the third kind? Is there a first kind and a second kind? Yep.

1. A close encounter of the **first kind** is the sighting of one or more UFOs.

2. A close encounter of the **second kind** is the observation of a UFO along with physical effects like paralysis or interference on radio or TV reception.

3. A close encounter of the **third kind** is the observation of some sort of alien being alongside the spotting of a UFO.

4. A close encounter of the **fourth kind** is the serious one—abduction!

ROSWELL, 1947

The Roswell incident is the most famous UFO incident ever. On July 8, 1947, Roswell Army Air Field (RAAF) reported that they had recovered a crashed "flying disk"—then later that same day said they reported that they had actually just found a weather balloon. Mysterious? People forgot all about the incident until 1978, when Major Jesse Marcel, who had been involved with the recovery at the crash site, said they had actually found an alien spacecraft. And so, the conspiracy theory was born! The truth is out there!

RESTRICTED AREA

AREA 51

- Top-secret military base located in Nevada. It's about 80 miles (128 km) south of Las Vegas.
- The base does not appear on US government maps. In fact, the government denied its very existence until 2000.
- Theorists claim that the base is used for the storage and study of alien spacecraft that have crashed to Earth, including the material found at Roswell.
- The highway that runs alongside Area 51 has been officially designated as the Extraterrestrial Highway by Nevada.

"If you look into the sky in the early morning you see them playing tag between the stars."
– Muhammad Ali

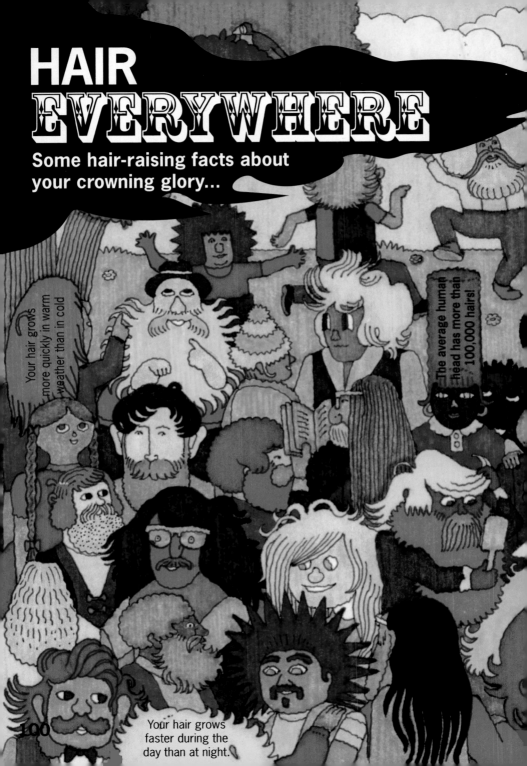

HAIR
EVERYWHERE

**Some hair-raising facts about
your crowning glory...**

Your hair grows more quickly in warm weather than in cold

The average human head has more than 100,000 hairs!

Your hair grows faster during the day than at night.

The average lifespan of a human hair is 5 years.

By the age of 50, more than 50 percent of men are balding.

Your hair grows about ½ inch (1.25 cm) a month.

Hair is mostly made up of keratin, the same stuff as your fingernails.

On average, 00 hairs a day fall from your scalp.

The longest beard on record belonged to Norwegian-born Hans Lanseth. At its longest, his beard was 17½ ft (5.3 m) long!

You're alone in a dark room with only a gas lamp, a wood stove, and a candle. You have only one match. What do you light first?

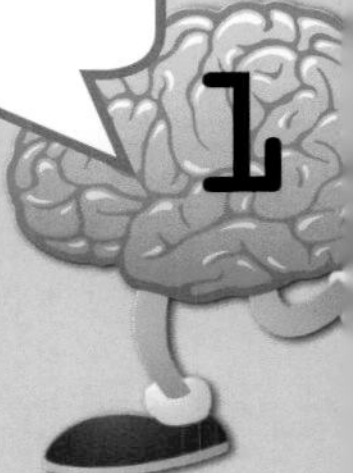

1

Billy's mother had four children. The first was named April, the second was named May, and the third was named June. What was the name of her fourth child?

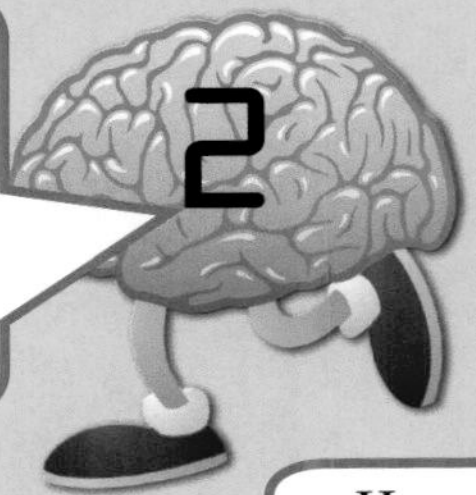

2

How can you use the letters in NEW DOOR to make one word?

The Mississippi River is the dividing line between Arkansas and Tennessee. If an airplane crashed smack bang in the middle of the Mississippi River, on which side would the survivors be buried?

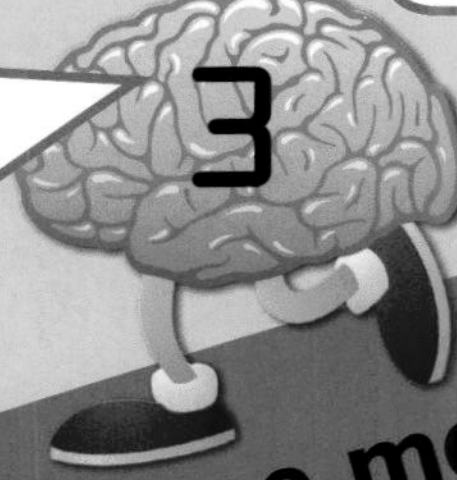

3

Let's do some mental exercises

MIND

ACTION FIGURE
Collector

The world's love affair with action figures began in 1964, when Hassenfeld Brothers (known today as Hasbro) unveiled a line of 12-inch, fully articulated G. I. Joe Action Soldiers. They were basically Barbie dolls for boys, and came complete with vehicles and accessories. Then, in 1977, the action-figure industry changed with the release of a little movie called Star Wars. Toy company Kenner released smaller 3¾ inch figures, which were so popular they became the new standard.

KNOW YOUR ACTION FIGURE LINGO!

Articulation—The movable parts and joints on an action figure.

Die Cast—Any toy made out of metal.

Blister—The clear (and often frustratingly difficult to open) clear plastic shell that encases the action figure.

MOC—Mint on card; this means the figure is unopened. What a shame!

Loose—Any toy that's no longer in its original packaging.

Shortpack—Action figures that are deliberately sold in reduced quantities. In each shipment, there's usually one shortpacked action figure per case. Toy companies do this to create demand for the shortpacked figure and make it worth more money.

The Most Expensive Action Figure Ever
Nothing beats an original. Created by Don Levine, the prototype for the original 1963 G. I. Joe sold to collector Steve Geppi for $200,000 in 2003!

Tantalizing Toy Fact
During the 1978 holiday season, Kenner sold over 42 million Star Wars action figures!

THE RATING GAME

The quality and condition of boxed action figures is rated on something called the "C" scale.

C10: Perfection, and incredibly rare.

C9: Very few defects. Excellent collector-quality toys.

C8.5: Very good condition, but collectors may avoid them.

C8: Visible flaws. The lowest collector-grade rating.

C6/7: Apparent flaws. Not for collectors—just for fun.

C5 and lower: Very poor quality Well-worn with large parts missing.

BE AN ACTION FIGURE

Collecting Star Wars and other action figures is cool and all, but what if you were the action figure? Today, it's possible. There are plenty of companies on the internet who will sculpt a custom action figure of you. You can even add cool stuff like voice capabilities, custom clothes, tattoos, and crazy accessories. You just need to provide the photo.

LONGEST, SHORTEST,

LONGEST HOT DOG
In 1996, Sara Lee made the world's longest hot dog, at 1,996 ft (608 m)—but there was no continuous bun to go with it so, sorry, no record! The record belongs to Shizuoka Meat Producers of Shizuoka, Japan, with a 1,969 ft (600 m) long wiener in a bun.

HIGHEST KETCHUP BOTTLE
The world's tallest ketchup bottle resides in Collinsville, Illinois. It's 170 ft (52 m) high—try giving that a shake!

HIGHEST MOUNTAIN
Mount Everest in the Himalayas is 29,035 ft (8,848 m).

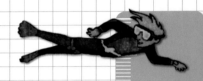

LONGEST RECORDED PROJECTILE VOMIT
is 27 ft (8 m). That's just short of the long jump world record.

DEEPEST SPOT IN THE OCEAN
The Mariana Trench in the Pacific Ocean is approximately 35,797 ft (10,910 m) deep. That's deeper than the height of Mount Everest!

LONGEST RIVER
The Nile River in Egypt is the world's longest river. It's 4,145 miles (6,671 km) long.

DEEPEST, HIGHEST

SHORTEST ESCALATOR
Located in Kawasaki More's department store in Japan, the world's shortest escalator is only 3⅓ in (8.43 cm) high!

LONGEST CONGA LINE
On March 13, 1998, in Miami, 119,986 people joined together in one gigantic conga line, setting the world record.

HIGHEST HOUSE OF CARDS
Card stacker Bryan Berg set the world record for highest house of cards, with a monstrous 25 ft 3½ in (7.7 m) card mansion. It took 2,400 decks to build it. Well it's cheaper than bricks and mortar!

SHORTEST RIVER
According to the Guinness Book of World Records, the Roe River in Great Falls, Montana, is the world's tiniest. It's only 200 ft (60 m) long.

HIGHEST WATERFALL
Angel Falls in Canaima National Park, Venezuela, is the highest waterfall in the world, at 3,212 ft (980 m).

LONGEST CAR
Jay Ohrberg designed the world's longest car—a 100 ft (30 m) limo that has 26 wheels. It even has two steering wheels, one at each end to help it back up! It comes equipped with a Jacuzzi, helipad, sundeck, and swimming pool (including diving board)!

WEIRD

In Canada, you can't pay for a fifty-cent item with only pennies.

In England, it's illegal to hang a bed out of a window.

In France, it's against the law to die unless you've already purchased a cemetery plot.

In Mexico, you can't lift either foot off the pedals while riding a bicycle because you might lose control.

LAWS

In Switzerland, it's against the law to flush the toilet after 10 o'clock at night.

In Thailand, it's illegal to leave your house if you're not wearing underwear.

In Australia, you can't wear hot-pink pants past 4 o'clock on a Sunday.

In Israel, it's against the law to bring a bear to the beach.

In Australia, taxi cabs must carry a bale of hay in their trunks at all times.

BIGFEET, YETIS, SASQUATCHES, AND SNOWMEN

Bigfoot, also known as Sasquatch, is a large apelike creature that supposedly prowls the Pacific Northwest region of North America. No hard evidence has ever been found that proves the existence of such a creature. In 1967, two men claimed to have captured footage of Bigfoot in California. Their short film clip is the best evidence that Bigfoot exists. But the recording is grainy and many people claim it's a hoax. Other similar creatures are said to inhabit other parts of the world. For example, the Yeti (also known as the Abominable Snowman), roams the Himalayan region of Nepal.

MYSTERIOUS
MYSTE

SOME THINGS IN LIFE CAN'T BE EXPLAINED... BUT
ARE A FEW FAMOUS MYSTERIOUS THAT HAVE

MISSING PLANES AND BOATS

The Bermuda Triangle (also known as the Devil's Triangle), is a section of the Atlantic Ocean between Florida, Bermuda, and San Juan in Puerto Rico. A vast number of planes and boats have disappeared in this area with no explanation at all. Some people claim it's haunted, others suspect that aliens have visited the spot, while others put it down to a time-travel portal.

The most infamous Bermuda Triangle incident is the story of the USS *Cyclops*. In 1918, the ship and its entire crew of 309 went missing in the Bermuda Triangle. They were never found.

A MUMMY'S CURSE?

King Tut's tomb is one of the most fascinating discoveries of our time. But could there be a curse surrounding it? The mystery began just weeks after the opening of the tomb, when Lord Carnarvon, the man who funded the exploration, died. It was said that all the lights of Cairo went out the instant he passed away.

Speculation only increased when it was revealed that inside the tomb an inscription was found on a shrine of Anubis, the god of the dead, which read "It is I who hinder the sand from choking the secret chamber. I am for the protection of the deceased."

RIES

THEY DO MAKE GREAT STORIES. HERE PERPLEXED HUMANKIND.

Years after, newspapers continued to report the deaths of those related to the discovery of the tomb. So could there really be a curse?

A MISSING CIVILIZATION?

Atlantis is a legendary island that was first mentioned in the writings of the Greek philosopher Plato. In his account, Atlantis was a beautiful island society that prospered around 9600 BCE. But, after its people tried to invade Athens, the island sank into the ocean, never to be seen again. Dozens of possible locations for the city have been suggested, including, Santorini in Greece, the Azores in the Atlantic, and off the coast of Cornwall in England.

ANCIENT EGYPT

The story of ancient Egypt

Around 5,000 years ago farmers first began to settle along the Nile River. After a time, two separate kingdoms developed there— Upper Egypt and Lower Egypt. In 3200 BCE the pharaoh of Upper Egypt conquered Lower Egypt and the kingdom was united. This was the true beginning of ancient Egypt. The society prospered for the next 3,000 years, until it was conquered by the Romans in 31 BCE.

King Tut's tomb

In 1922, British archeologist Howard Carter discovered Tutankhamun's (King Tut's) tomb. It was almost perfectly preserved and was full of treasure, including a solid gold mask of King Tut's face. Today, King Tut is one of the most famous of all the ancient Egyptian pharaohs, but he was actually a pretty unimportant ruler. He became pharaoh when he was only 9 and died when he was just 18.

The Nile life

Most ancient Egyptians were farmers. They lived in mud-brick houses that kept them cool under the hot Egyptian sun. Every year the Nile would flood and the farmers would plant their crops in the fertile flood banks.

EGYPTRIVIA!

⏵ The ancient Egyptians believed fried mice would cure a toothache.

⏵ Pharaohs never let their hair be seen—so they would always wear a headdress.

⏵ The ancient Egyptians invented makeup!

By the gods!

The ancient Egyptians worshiped over 2,000 gods! Their gods and goddesses were often represented by a human with the head of an animal. One of the most famous Egyptian gods was Ra, the Sun god. He wore a mask of a falcon, with a sun disk balanced on top.

Mummies

When you think of Egypt, you probably think of mummies. A mummy is a body that has been preserved after death. The ancient Egyptians mummified human bodies because they believed it would help them have a safe voyage into the afterlife. Because mummification was expensive, the richer someone was, the better mummified they would be and the more complex their burial. A well-mummified body would be preserved for much longer.

The pyramids

The Pyramids were giant tombs built for the pharaohs. The three pyramids of Giza, near Cairo, are still standing and Khufu's pyramid, the largest of the three, is considered one of the seven wonders of the ancient world. In fact, Khufu's Pyramid, also known as the Great Pyramid of Giza, was the tallest building in the world for 5,000 years until the Eiffel Tower was built in 1889.

EWW! Disgusting facts about gruesome things

A selection of squishy, slimy, and utterly disgusting facts about really gross things.

On average, people swallow 14 insects a year while they sleep! Talk about a midnight feast... Yuk!

Sixty-five percent of nose pickers use their index finger.

A cockroach can live for nine days without its head.

You swallow about one quart (0.95 liters) of mucus and snot every day. Yum.

Many popular brands of yogurt and gelatin dessert contain pork gelatin. We're all for hot-dog-flavored yogurt—right?

1 lb (450g) of peanut butter can contain up to 5 rodent hairs and 150 bug fragments. You might want to leave the peanut butter out of your next PB&J sandwich.

In ancient Rome, when men played in the Olympic games, they did it entirely naked.

A single pair of rats can produce 15,000 descendents in a year—and 20 million in three years.

Parasites count for 0.01 percent of your body weight.

The average person's bed is home to over 6 billion dust mites. That's gross 6 billion ways.

People fart an average of **14 TIMES** a day.

The world record for eating live maggots is 100 in less than 5½ minutes.

TWIN-TUITION? Could twins actually have extra sensory perception (ESP)? Well, no one seems to know for sure. Science says no. But there are countless sets of twins who claim they share some sort of paranormal connection. The most common examples of "twin-tuition" are things like finishing each other's sentences, knowing what the other twin is thinking, and even feeling each other's pain.

THE JIM TWINS: There are many cases of twins being separated at birth, only to meet years later and discover how similar they are. The most extreme example is the "Jim Twins." Jim Lewis and Jim Springer were adopted by separate families when they were just one month old. They reunited when they were 39 and they couldn't believe the amazing things they had in common...
• They had both been married twice—both first wives were named Linda and both second wives were named Betty.
• One Jim named his son James Allen—the other named his son James Alan.
• They had both been employed as sheriffs, and both chewed their fingernails.

IDENTICAL TWINS have virtually the same DNA—but not the same fingerprints. So if you have an identical twin, you can't frame them for stealing the cookies from the cookie jar!

The fancy science word for identical twins is **MONOZYGOTIC**. Fraternal twins are called **DIZYGOTIC**.

ELVIS PRESLEY WAS A TWIN but his sibling died at birth.

MOST TWINS ARE BORN ON THE SAME DAY but they don't have to be! The longest gap between twin birth dates is 85 days.

TWINS OCCUR IN OTHER SPECIES BESIDES HUMANS, most commonly in cats, sheep, deer, and ferrets. In fact, one species of armadillo has litters of identical quadruplets as its regular method of reproduction.

TWINS

Best things ever said about POLITICS

"Before I refuse to take your questions, I have an opening statement."

Ronald Reagan, US President (1981–89)

"You're working hard to put food on your family."

George W. Bush, US President (2001–09)

"Politics, it seems to me, for years, or all too long, has been concerned with right or left, instead of right or wrong."

Richard Armour, poet

"Democracy is being allowed to vote for the candidate you dislike least."

Robert Byrne, author

"Solutions are not the answer."

Richard Nixon, US President (1969–74)

"Politics, n: [Poly "many" + tics "blood-sucking parasites"]"

Larry Hardiman

"Any American who is prepared to run for president should automatically, by definition, be disqualified from ever doing so."

Gore Vidal, author

"Whenever I hear anyone arguing for slavery, I feel a strong impulse to see it tried on him personally."

Abraham Lincoln,
US President (1861–65)

"I have come to the conclusion that politics is too serious a matter to be left to the politicians."

Charles de Gaulle, President of France (1959–69)

"If you haven't found something worth dying for, you aren't fit to be living."

Martin Luther King, Jr.

"Ask not what your country can do for you; ask what you can do for your country."

John Fitzgerald Kennedy,
US President (1961–63)

"Being powerful is like being a lady. If you have to tell people you are, you aren't."

Margaret Thatcher, British Prime Minister (1979–90)

MEGAWORDS

Want to impress your friends with really, really, really, really, really long words... and know what they mean. Here's a long list!

Hippopotomonstrosesquipedaliophobia
Some wordsmith out there has a good sense of humor. This super-long word means "the fear of long words."

Misodoctakleidist
Someone who hates playing the piano.

Nash-gob
Someone who gossips.

Floccinaucinihilipilification
This was the longest word to appear in the first edition of the Oxford English Dictionary. It's defined as "the action or habit of estimating as worthless."

Honorificabilitudinitatibus

In 1721, this was recognized as the longest word in the English language. It's just a really, really long way of saying "honorableness" or "having honor."

Humuhumunukunukuapua'a

A Hawaiian fish. It's been said that the name is longer than the fish.

Chargoggagoggmanchauggagoggchaubunagungamaugg

This monster name refers to a lake in Massachusetts. It's literally translated as "I'll fish on the right side, you fish on the left side, no one fishes in the middle."

Trichophagia

The extremely unhealthy habit of eating a lot of hair.

Squirreled

This is the longest one-syllable word in the English language. It means to store or hide.

BUILD A

BUILD YOUR OWN

EVER WONDERED HOW GREAT IT WOULD BE TO FIND YOUR OWN BURIED TREASURE? WHY NOT MAKE YOUR OWN!

HOW LONG?

First step—decide how long you want it to remain unopened. You can go for one year, 10, or even 50 years and see how much things have changed. Or, you could leave if for 500 years, ready to be discovered by an alien leader.

THE CAPSULE

The container you use to create the capsule will depend on where you put it. So, to bury or not to bury? That is the question. If you want to dig a hole, find a box that won't rot or decay in the ground—it has to be waterproof.

ALMOST DONE

OK, you're almost finished. On the front, write in big, bold letters DO NOT OPEN UNTIL such-and-such date. Then bury or hide it, and forget about it—but not totally, or you'll forget to find it.

WHAT TO INCLUDE

Whatever you want! Here are a few suggestions:
- Magazine clippings
- Photos of you and your family
- A letter to your future self
- Popular toys
- Labels from your favorite foods.

Put everything in individual bags.

WHAT NOT TO INCLUDE

- Food of any kind—as tempted as you might be to see what a banana would look like 10 years from now, don't do it!
- Anything liquid.
- Anything with a strong odor (especially if you're going to bury it—you'll attract all the neighborhood dogs!).

IT WILL MAKE YOU FEEL LIKE A PIRATE FROM THE MOVIES, HIDING YOUR TREASURE

"A **time capsule** is anything that saves stuff with the intention of being found and opened at a later time. The modern idea of a planned time capsule has been around since the 1930s."

Register that bad boy! If you want to be official, register your time capsule. You can write to the **International Time Capsule Society** at: International Time Capsule Society, Oglethorpe University, 4484 Peachtree Road NE Atlanta, GA 30319-2797.

TIME CAPSULE

TIME CAPSULE FACTS!

BURYING YOUR TIME CAPSULE CAN BE PROBLEMATIC! Need proof? The town of Corona, California, has lost track of 17 buried time capsules!

The Crypt of Civilization at Oglethorpe University in Atlanta is generally considered to be THE FIRST SUCCESSFUL, ORGANIZED BURIED TIME CAPSULE. It was built in 1936 and isn't scheduled to be opened for THOUSANDS of years—8,113, to be exact. Inside is a Bible, a machine to teach the English language, and, last but not least, SOME BUDWEISER BEER.

The phrase "time capsule" was first coined in 1937. Originally, the term was going to be "time bomb." Then someone realized that this sounded a little scary and switched it to time capsule. (If you discovered something in the ground with the words TIME BOMB written on it, would you really want to open it?)

.

There's actually an International Time Capsule Society that keeps a database of every time capsule on the planet.

"There are 1,400 time capsule groups registered worldwide and they estimate that there are nearly 15,000 time capsules spread across the world. Sadly, they think 80% of all time capsules are forgotten.

PRIVATE DO NOT OPEN

APRIL FOOLS' FOOLS

APRIL 1ST. What a day! Pranks and jokes abound. Here are a few classics from April Fools' Days past…

Bombs Away!

It was 1915, the middle of World War I, when a French pilot flew over a German camp and dropped what looked like a giant bomb. The German soldiers thought they were done for. But there was no explosion. They approached the bomb and discovered it was actually a soccer ball, with a note attached that read "April Fools!"

Big Digital Ben

On April 1, 1980, the BBC reported that the most famous clock in the world, London's Big Ben, would be switching to a digital readout in order to keep up with the times. British folks were furious, until the BBC let them in on the joke.

Wasps Are Coming!

In 1949, a New Zealand radio DJ announced that a mile-wide swarm of wasps was heading for Auckland. He urged everyone to leave honey traps outside their homes and to wear their socks over their pants, so that no flesh was exposed. The New Zealand Broadcasting Service didn't think the joke was funny and to this day a warning memo is sent out every year before April Fools' Day.

White Doggies
In 1965, a Copenhagen newspaper reported that the Danish parliament had passed a bizarre new law requiring all dogs to be painted white so that they would be seen more easily at night. Whether or not anyone actually painted their dog white—well, we can only imagine.

Lefty Burger
In 1998, Burger King ran an ad in USA Today announcing the brand new Left-Handed Whopper—a burger with the ketchup, cheese, and all the other condiments switched 180 degrees for left-handed burger eaters. Thousands of customers ran to Burger King requesting lefty burgers.

The Swiss Spaghetti Harvest
In 1957, the BBC news program Panorama proclaimed that, thanks to the "virtual disappearance of the spaghetti weevil," the year's Swiss spaghetti crop would be bigger than ever. A video showed Swiss farmers pulling spaghetti from trees. People believed it! Viewers called the BBC, asking how to grow their own. The BBC responded, "place a sprig of spaghetti in a can of tomato sauce and hope for the best."

Look Ma, No Gravity
In 1976, British astronomer Patrick Moore went on BBC radio and announced that a once-in-a-lifetime astronomical event was about to occur. Pluto was going to pass behind Jupiter, causing a gravitational shift that would briefly reduce Earth's own gravity. Moore told listeners that if they jumped at the exact moment it occurred, they'd be able to float in the air for a moment. Hundreds of people tried it—some even calling the BBC to say that it worked!

ANSWERS

P24—25 Who Am I?

WHO? Walt Disney
WHERE? Eiffel Tower
WHAT? Typewriter

P27 Wonders of the World

Great Pyramid of Giza
Hanging Gardens of Babylon
Temple of Artemis at Ephesus
Statue of Zeus at Olympia
Mausoleum of Maussollos at Halicarnassus
Colossus of Rhodes
Lighthouse of Alexandria

P28—29 Brainteasers

1. Just one, then it isn't empty anymore.
2. He escaped in the winter, when the water surrounding the island had frozen. He walked across the ice.
3. They weren't playing against each other.
4. The man was bald.
5. Short (shorter).
6. 31,536,000 (or in a leap year—31,622,400.)
7. They were a grandfather, father, and son.

P60 Scaly!

Antarctica. It's too cold.

P62 Phobias

- Telephonophobia—Fear of telephones
- Amnesiphobia—Fear of amnesia
- Nudophobia—Fear of nudity
- Somniphobia—Fear of sleep
- Carnophobia—Fear of meat
- Bibliophobia—Fear of books

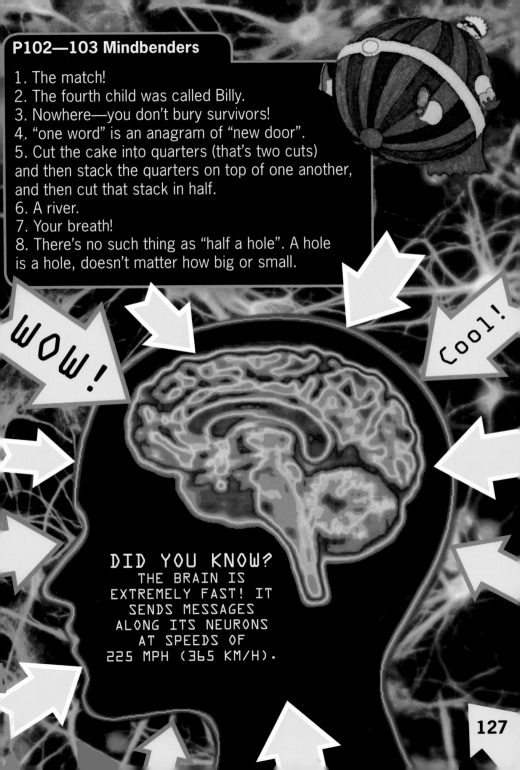

P102—103 Mindbenders

1. The match!
2. The fourth child was called Billy.
3. Nowhere—you don't bury survivors!
4. "one word" is an anagram of "new door".
5. Cut the cake into quarters (that's two cuts) and then stack the quarters on top of one another, and then cut that stack in half.
6. A river.
7. Your breath!
8. There's no such thing as "half a hole". A hole is a hole, doesn't matter how big or small.

WOW!

Cool!

DID YOU KNOW?
THE BRAIN IS EXTREMELY FAST! IT SENDS MESSAGES ALONG ITS NEURONS AT SPEEDS OF 225 MPH (365 KM/H).

ACKNOWLEDGMENTS

Max Brallier would like to thank Abby, for putting up with him. With love.

Dorling Kindersley would like to thank Fleur Star for her editorial help; and Clemence Monot, Emma Forge, and Tom Forge for their design assistance.

The publisher would like to thank the following for their kind permission to reproduce their photographs:

(Key: a-above; b-below/bottom; c-center; f-far; l-left; r-right; t-top)

Alamy Images: Andy Ennis 105tr; Mary Evans Picture Library 8cr; National Motor Museum / Motoring Picture Library 18br; PhotoStock-Israel 104bl. **Walt Anthony:** 70cr. **Corbis:** Danny Lehman 54-55 (background); Louie Psihoyos 19r. **DK Images:** Robert L. Braun - modelmaker 10cb, 10ftr; The British Museum 112-113; Centaur Studios - modelmakers 10-11c; Coca Cola 8fclb; Graham High at Centaur Studios - modelmaker 11ca; Sean Hunter 55bl; Imperial War Museum, Duxford 9ftr; London Planetarium 76fcr; Jamie Marshall 55fcla; Judith Miller / Cooper Owen 9clb; Judith Miller / Noel Barrett Antiques & Auctions Ltd 9tc; NASA 76fcrb, 98ftl; NASA / Finley Holiday Films 77fbr, 99c; Stephen Oliver 34cr, 34crb, 34fbl, 34fcl, 34fcr, 35fbr, 55br; Luis Rey - modelmaker 10cl; Rough Guides 54fbr, 54fcl, 55cla; Royal Tyrrell Museum of Palaeontology, Alberta, Canada 11bl; Jerry Young 18bl. **FLPA:** Steven Ruiter / FN / Minden 19crb. **Getty Images:** De Agostini Picture Library / DEA / W. Buss 54clb; fStop / Halfdark 36tl, 37br; Ciaran Griffin / Stockbyte 18tc; Iconica / Arctic-Images 10-11 (background); Illustration Works / Dietrich Madsen 56-57b; The Image Bank / Ed Freeman 54crb; Photographer's Choice / Chris Collins 94-95 (border); Andy Rouse / The Image Bank 19br; Stockbyte / John Foxx 94-95 (background); Stocktrek RF 78fbl, 79cl, 79fbr, 79tr; Taxi / James Porto 78-79; Visuals Unlimited / Ken Lucas 11br; Toru Yamanaka / AFP 18cla. **iStockphoto.com:**

Mads Abildgaard 28-29; Apatrimonio 44-45c; Arlindo71 88fclb (ant); Mike Bentley 32-33 (background); Matjaz Boncina 36-37 (background); James Bowyer 60cb, 61clb, 61tr; Jens Carsten 70bl; CostinT 66-67; Cyfrogclone 42-43 (background / soda cup); Julie de Leseleuc 44cl, 44clb, 45fbr, 45ftr; David Dea 52bl; Hywit Dimyadi 125tc; Gabriela Durán 44c; Hannah Eckman 40clb; Jamie Farrant 110-111; Julie Felton 102c (brain), 102ca (brain), 102cra (brain), 102fbl (brain), 103br (brain), 103cla (brain), 103fbr (brain), 103fcl (brain), 103fcrb (brain), 103tr (brain); Graffizone 118bc, 118bl, 118-119b; KarlKotas Inc. 32cra; KateLeigh 72bl, 73br, 73fcla; Attila Kis 71tl; Sergey Krivoruchko 71bl; Abel Leão 114-115; Liangpv 108-109t; Bill Noll 22-23 (background); Skip O'Donnell 28fclb, 29tl; Kirsty Pargeter 46-47; Pavlen 92tl; Plainview 58-59 (background); RTimages 3c; RussellTatedotCom 104-105 (background); Anssi Ruuska 109ftr; Saw 40tl, 68-69 (background); Scibak 108ftl (window); Chris Scredon 64 (background), 65 (background); Simon2579 118-119 (background); Dieter Spears 118-119c; Song Speckels 44tc; SpiffyJ 71cr; Mark Stay 102c (legs), 102ca (legs), 102cra (legs), 102fbl (legs), 103br (legs), 103cla (legs), 103fbr (legs), 103fcl (legs), 103fcrb (legs), 103tr (legs); Stocksnapper 1cb; Tomograf 93tr; Hans Van Ijzendoorn 93cra; Kristina Velickovic 42-43 (background / ice creams); Graça Victoria 88fclb (cake); Klara Viskova 46fbl, 47fbr; John Woodcock 48c, 48tl; Serdar Yagci 60-61 (background); Robertas Pižas 88-89 (background). **National Geographic Stock:** Stephen Alvarez 76-77 (background). **Rex Features:** South West News Service 19cra. **Science Photo Library:** Robert Gendler 98-99 (background); Nancy Kedersha 126-127 (background); Pasieka 127cb.

All other images © Dorling Kindersley
For further information see:
www.dkimages.com

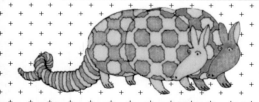